What people are saying about …

RELAUNCH

"Having led a major turnaround myself, I can declare with certainty that it is a tough job. Mark Rutland has led three, and *ReLaunch* is the result. Every leader needs this insightful and powerful book."

Mike Huckabee, former Arkansas governor and host of the number-one rated weekend hit *HUCKABEE* on the Fox News Channel

"When I think of turnaround leadership, I think of Mark Rutland. He is one of the most effective communicators I have heard in fifty years of ministry. His rich experience and engaging style make *ReLaunch* an absolute gold mine for leaders."

James Robison, president of LIFE Outreach International in Fort Worth, Texas

"Dr. Mark Rutland's new book, *ReLaunch*, is a must-read for all leaders. Whether you need to turn your organization around or take it further than it's been before, this book gives you the tools to lead your business to success."

Jentezen Franklin, senior pastor of Free Chapel and *New York Times* best-selling author of *Fasting*

"Dr. Rutland truly has a lifetime's worth of experience leading organizations on the verge of collapse—a church, a college, and a university—and bringing them back from the brink. And the leadership lessons he imparts in this book are invaluable. Whether you've been a leader for years or are just starting out, I highly recommend reading this book from cover to cover!"

Robert Morris, founding senior pastor of Gateway Church and best-selling author of *The Blessed Life, The God I Never Knew,* and *The Blessed Church*

"Balancing his firm grip on an organization's needs with his loose personal hold on position, Mark offers leaders a practical insider's view of meaningful turnaround. In the university world, Mark has been on the front edge of those who do it right, so I'm thankful he has written this no-holds-bared gritty guide for godly turnaround success. Those who are facing tough challenges finally have in this book the insights they need to unleash the joy of leading those they serve out of the valley of despair and into a future of fulfilling God's best for their ministries."

Dr. Roger Parrott, president of Belhaven University and author of *The Longview*

RELAUNCH

HOW TO STAGE AN ORGANIZATIONAL COMEBACK

DR. MARK RUTLAND
PRESIDENT OF ORAL ROBERTS UNIVERSITY

David C Cook®
transforming lives together

RELAUNCH
Published by David C Cook
4050 Lee Vance View
Colorado Springs, CO 80918 U.S.A.

David C Cook Distribution Canada
55 Woodslee Avenue, Paris, Ontario, Canada N3L 3E5

David C Cook U.K., Kingsway Communications
Eastbourne, East Sussex BN23 6NT, England

The graphic circle C logo is a registered trademark of David C Cook.

The website addresses recommended throughout this book are offered as a
resource to you. These websites are not intended in any way to be or imply an
endorsement on the part of David C Cook, nor do we vouch for their content.

LCCN 2012953800
ISBN 978-1-4347-0575-4
eISBN 978-0-7814-0959-9

© 2013 Mark Rutland

The Team: Don Pape, Barbara Dycus, Amy Konyndyk, Caitlyn Carlson, Karen Athen
Cover Design: Nick Lee

Printed in the United States of America
First Edition 2013

3 4 5 6 7 8 9 10

021913

CONTENTS

Acknowledgments   7

Foreword   9

Preface   11

PART I: LEARNING THE ART OF LEADERSHIP

1. My Mother's Flower Beds   17

2. Dream Day and Mrs. Burkett   23

3. My Turnaround Leadership Journey   29

4. Before the Nuts and Bolts: Leadership as an Art   53

PART II: THE SEVEN STEPS OF THE TURNAROUND

5. Step 1: Facing Institutional Reality   71

6. Step 2: Communicating a Vision   87

7. Step 3: Aligning Market, Message, and Medium   101

8. Step 4: Creating an Executable Strategy   113

9. Step 5: Shifting Culture   127

10. Step 6: Keeping an Eye on Quality   145

11. Step 7: Measuring and Celebrating Success   153

PART III: BUILDING THE TURNAROUND TEAM

12. Hiring for a Turnaround   161

13. The Troubling Art of Firing   173

14. Forming a Board   183

Epilogue: The Inner Life of the Turnaround Leader   197

Notes   205

ACKNOWLEDGMENTS

Apparently incapable of embarrassment, as only Claude Rains could have played him, the unabashedly "flexible" Captain Renault, standing over Major Strasser's body, orders his officers to, "Round up the usual suspects." Some authors' acknowledgements seem to do only that. As a result they seem more obligatory than truly grateful. May these few words somehow be spared that taint. To the vast catalogue of my failings I am loath to add ingratitude.

I am truly, deeply grateful to all those who made this project—and it was a project—possible. To my cherished wife, Alison, who sweetly coaxed me back to writing after a recess that lasted way too long. To my son-in-law, James Leatherbarrow, who spent countless hours in reading, rereading, editing, and dealing with administrative details. To Stephen and Beverly Mansfield. To David C Cook Publishers, who saw merit and brought the book to life.

Thank you all. My most sincere thanks. Far from usual, you were all unusually diligent, unusually faithful, and unusually encouraging.

FOREWORD

I'm a big fan of Mark Rutland and his book *ReLaunch*. Why? Because he's a man who lives and teaches simple truths.

With change being a way of life today, every leader of note will have to be able to turn around an organization sometime in his or her career. Below are some of the simple truths I learned from Mark's excellent book about this important subject.

If you want to relaunch an organization, you must:

1. Diagnose the truth about the present reality. What's happening, both good and bad, in the organization right now?
2. Given that reality, determine what is realistic about where you can take the organization. What is your vision?
3. Develop a strategy to get there. Who should be on the bus? What should you do first, second, and third? Where will the money come from to do it all?
4. Determine ways to measure progress. How will you know when you are there?
5. Involve everyone who can impact the results. Then praise progress, redirect undesirable pathways, and celebrate victories—both small and large.
6. Keep on keeping on—the journey is never over.

These observations and their ordering are in my words, but all of them are motivated by Mark's thinking.

Does the fact that I said these are simple truths mean turning around an organization is easy? Not by a long shot! It's tough. It will take a toll on you, your family, your health, and your ego. Is it worth it? Yes. Somebody has to do it, or the organization will die and everyone will be out on the street.

Mark's style, his use of real-life *laboratories of leadership*, his practical application, and his insightful historical illustrations also make this an extremely readable book.

Read *ReLaunch*, and learn from Mark Rutland's wisdom. Then put your right hand on your left shoulder and your left hand on your right shoulder and give yourself a hug. You are going to be a person to be admired.

—Ken Blanchard
Coauthor of *The One Minute Manager*,
Leading at a Higher Level, and *Lead Like Jesus*

PREFACE

With a gut-wrenching scream of metal on rock, the Italian cruise liner *Costa Concordia* ran aground off the coast of Italy at 9:45 p.m. on January 13, 2012. More than thirty lives were lost, the ship was wrecked, and Captain Francesco Schettino's life and career were destroyed. The cause of the wreck was apparently arrogant and distracted leadership. But the worst part of the *Costa Concordia* story may actually be what happened after the ship hit the rocks. In fact, the wreck of the *Costa Concordia* is a study in bad crisis leadership. Selfish senior leadership in denial and a confused, unprepared, and perhaps even cowardly staff combined to create a horror story for the passengers.

The *Costa Concordia* was not the first ship to run aground. Nor will it be the last. It may well have been the poorest in history at handling the crisis. Businesses, organizations, and even churches hit the rocks. So do lives. Some wrecks are terminal. They simply cannot be saved. Salvaged and sold for scrap or abandoned to lie forever on the ocean floor, they are finished. This book is not about such wrecks as those. Nor is it a forensic study of terminal wrecks, their causes, and who is to blame. Let someone else deal with the pathology of the hapless Captain Schettino.

My concern here is to say that not every crisis has to be fatal. In the history of most organizations—indeed, most lives—there are seasons of decline or at least a dead calm, a time when doubt sets in and the doomsday forecasters circle like buzzards. This book is a word of encouragement to the leader or leaders whose job it is to get the wreck off the rocks and relaunch her. Someone has to come aboard and restore calm. Someone has to nudge the ship off the reef without ripping out the hull. Someone has to weed out those of the crew who refuse to be renewed in the spirit of servant-leadership. Someone has to model and demand from all hands a genuine concern for saving the ship, the crew, and the passengers. That same someone has to repaint, remodel, and eventually set back out to sea. There is a sublime reward reserved for the few who will take on the hard, dangerous work of turnaround leadership. This book is for the gutsy servant-leader who thrives on that splendid moment when he summons all hands on deck for an announcement: "This ship can sail again, will sail again, faster and safer because we have lived over this wreck and learned from it. This ship is not as good as new. It is better because we are better." That kind of a relaunch is a marvelous thing to see. A ship rising from the graveyard of the ocean to sail once again is glorious to behold. But it is costly and strenuous work and not for the faint of heart.

This book is for all who have the courage to lead an organization up and out of its winter of discontent. To be sure, it takes great leadership to step in and lead a winning team to new heights of glory. This book is just not about that. This book is for the rugged visionaries who see in the wreckage a hope for the future and are willing to pay the price for a relaunch.

My hat is off to them. And this book is theirs.

—Mark Rutland, 2012

You will be called Repairer of Broken Walls.

—Isaiah 58:12 NIV

PART I

LEARNING THE ART OF LEADERSHIP

CHAPTER ONE

MY MOTHER'S FLOWER BEDS

There is a memory that has come back to me time and again in my life, a memory that has informed much of what I believe about shaping organizations. On the surface this memory may not be very impressive, but over time it has inspired a great deal of what I now know about turnaround leadership.

In my early years, my father's work meant that our family moved often. Every time we pulled up stakes, we spoke little of what we were leaving behind. The party line was, "Excitement ahead! No grieving!" Not surprisingly, this made for an unsettled childhood. We were constantly on the move. I attended multiple schools each year until I went to college. I was always the new kid, and I always felt a little out of place. No matter how hard things were wherever we lived, I consoled myself that we would probably be gone by

Christmas anyway. I tended to put out vines rather than put down roots wherever I lived.

Despite these upheavals, I couldn't help but admire my mother's resilience. She endured the many moves with a calm that mystified me. I'm sure the challenge of a new town, a new house, and new arrangements for her children stressed her—but I never saw it. What I did see was that after we were settled in each new house, a day would come when Mother would eventually go out into the yard, kneel down, and start remaking the flower beds. Now, this didn't make much sense to me. The beds were a mess, and we would be leaving before long anyway. What was the point of improving anything? The question didn't seem to trouble her. Diligently, she worked in the dirt—pulling weeds, planting seeds, placing bright mums, training vines, bringing order out of chaos and care out of neglect. Every time we moved into a new rental house, out she went and got to work. And when it was time to leave, she willingly offered up the work she had done in those newly beautiful beds for the joy of the next tenant.

Her flower beds were my first exposure to the hard, rewarding work of a turnaround.

"Mom," I asked her once, "don't you get tired of moving from one rental house to another?"

Her answer has never left me. She said, "I never worry about how long we stay in one place as long as when I leave, the flower beds are in better shape than when I got there." That's turnaround leadership in a nutshell. You are not thinking primarily of your own experience. You are not letting your past keep you from your task. You simply make things better for those who come next. Your goal is to leave the flower beds in better shape than you found them.

Over the last nearly quarter of a century, I have had the privilege of leading the news-making turnarounds of three large organizations on the edge of collapse—a megachurch and two universities. Turnaround has become a specialty for me. I have studied it in history, practiced it in the three major phases of my career, and distilled its processes into the principles you are about to read. After all these years, I've come to this conclusion: what I call *turnaround leadership* is not something mystical, murky, or mysterious that only the especially gifted can do. I believe turnaround leadership is a skill—or, rather, a set of skills—that can be developed. It is a matter of vision—of seeing opportunity where everyone else sees an unmanageable mess, of tirelessly communicating a defining vision, and of making that vision a reality on the ground. It's complicated and difficult and usually exhausting, but it doesn't have to be out of reach for most of us.

I have seen masterful relaunches staged by hundreds of great leaders I have studied. Lee Iacocca, CEO of Chrysler in the 1980s, comes to mind. He knew how to inspire and how to command, how to repair the inner machinery of his company with boldness and skill. He also knew how to embody the culture of his corporation before the watching world. By the time he started appearing as Chrysler's spokesman on those famous television commercials, he had already completed one of the great corporate turnarounds in history. I also think of Steve Jobs. He was an unusual man, but there is little in the annals of leadership like his triumphant return to Apple, the company that he founded and that later fired him. As we all now know, he went on to create the iPod, the iPhone, and the iPad, and in doing so he turned Apple around—transforming a generation in the process. Now *that* is turnaround leadership!

There are also a lot of bad examples on the pages of leadership history. In the 1980s and '90s, "Chainsaw" Al Dunlap was the CEO of companies like Scott Paper and Sunbeam. Believing that business turnarounds were measured only in profits for shareholders, Dunlap routinely closed factories, squeezed operations, and turned the painful, humiliating mass layoff into a dreaded art form. He refashioned companies through a ruthless scorched-earth policy that left thousands of people unemployed and made *turnaround* a dirty word nationwide. He apparently thought he was a success because he emerged from all of this with a hundred-million-dollar golden parachute for himself. Dunlap didn't seem to care about the devastation he left behind until an SEC investigation revealed that his remarkable achievements were due more to accounting fraud than to astute management. The trials that ensued dragged on for years. Meanwhile, entire companies were driven into bankruptcy by his mythical brand of turnaround. His legacy? Several major business periodicals have included Dunlap on their list of the worst CEOs of all time. That is not servant leadership, and it is no way to make a turnaround.

Yet greatness is possible, and it has come to be nearly synonymous with a successful turnaround. Think of it: most of the people we call "great" in history were people who effected a strategic turn at a strategic time toward a strategic goal—Alfred the Great, Simon Bolivar, Abraham Lincoln, Mohandas K. Gandhi, Nelson Mandela, Winston Churchill, and David Ben-Gurion. Each of these had to summon a vision, summon a people to that vision, and summon wisdom to lead a nation up from disaster or decline.

In fact, this is one of the reasons I'm glad I first honed the craft of the turnaround in religious institutions. Frankly, there tends to be more wrongheadedness, more *magical thinking*, in faith-based institutions than in any other. Faith is good, of course. I'm a man of faith. But faith is no substitute for wise action. Often I had to overcome bad theology and wispy concepts of leadership to turn the ship. This allowed me to get a firm grasp on what works and to learn how to articulate what works in clear language. Each success I made thrilled me at the possibilities of turnaround leadership for our lives, our nation, and our world. I believe in it so completely that I've decided to devote the rest of my life to helping people master the power of strategic turnarounds.

There could not be a better time for it. We are living in a day in which nearly every human institution needs to be reimagined, reinvented, and relaunched—in short, turned around. We all know that our various levels of government are in desperate need of a return to first principles. We long for leaders who understand how to turn the ship of state toward her finest hour. Our industries need men and women who understand it is a new era, demanding a new kind of leadership skilled at creating new and creative corporate cultures. This means turnaround. Churches, schools, nonprofits, and businesses need turnarounds. In fact, if our nation responds to its present crises with the best it has to throw into the fight, I believe history may yet call us "the Turnaround Generation."

There is more, though, and to understand it you must recognize a maxim most people never apply. It is this: *if a principle of leadership is true, it is true for every kind of leadership.* Now, I'm not talking about the technical side of leadership—how to run an airport or direct a roomful of accountants. I'm talking about how to inspire, position, coach, and empower people to do what they are made to do as part of a larger team. Whatever is true of Sony in this regard is true of your softball team. Whatever is true of General Electric when it comes to turning organizations—which just means large bodies of people—is in many ways true of any relationship. In fact, I'm certain that many turnaround truths work in marriage, work in friendship, and even work in the way we direct ourselves from within—the way we orchestrate our lives according to certain values and goals.

I've been fortunate; I've had great turnaround success. In fact, more than one business writer has referred to me as a "worker of miracles." I can assure you, though, I am no miracle worker. The success I've had has come from being bold in the pursuit of a vision, implementing a plan, learning from my mistakes, and understanding what it takes to summon the best in people—not from just sitting around and hoping for a miracle.

You can do it too. Whatever your arena, whatever your gift, turnaround truths can help you reinvigorate and realign. It is an art we desperately need in these times, an art that is not the possession of geniuses alone, and an art we can master and transfer to the next generation.

CHAPTER TWO

DREAM DAY AND MRS. BURKETT

Before I tell you a bit of my turnaround history and before we consider even one detail of the turnaround art, I want to plant a seed in your mind. It may be the most important thing I do for you in this book.

Here is that seed: *leadership, and particularly turnaround leadership, is about defining a dream and tethering all aspects of the organization to it.* Some dream well. Some define well. Others may tether well or excel at organizing. The art, though—the great craft of leading others—is the connection between the dream, its proclamation, and making the dream the driving force of everything that is done.

I wish this could be taught. I wish that we could acquire it through statistics and research, seminars and training. All of these help, of course, but learning how to define a dream—the vision for a person or an organization—is one of those skills that combine a dozen gifts and fields all infused by intuition and even spiritual insight. It can be learned, but it cannot come from a book or a college course alone. It can be mastered, but usually only after experience, failure, mentoring, and repeated unsatisfying attempts.

This is why I'm taking the risk here of telling you a bit of my story. I have something of a reputation as an expert in turnaround leadership. Yet it would not serve you well if I simply began to tell you the processes of a turnaround without describing the experiences that allowed me to hone the craft, to move from textbook principle to practiced art.

When I was in the fifth grade, I had a teacher named Mrs. Burkett. My family was living in a mean little town somewhere in Florida. The school held kindergarten through twelfth grade in one shabby building. There were fights every day. It was a pretty scary place for an eleven-year-old *new kid* to try to fit in.

The saving grace was Mrs. Burkett. She was a short, rotund little woman, and she wasn't particularly well educated. In fact, she taught me a mispronunciation of *Mesopotamia* that came back to haunt me decades later when I was giving a talk at the University of Maryland. That's for another book. Whatever Mrs. Burkett's short-comings, she more than made up for them on the first Monday of every month.

On those Mondays at the unwelcoming little school, she would rub her chubby hands together and glance around the room with twinkling eyes. "Class," she'd say, "it's Dream Day!" Knowing what was coming, the students would quickly circle up their chairs and wait expectantly. And one by one, for as long as it took, we would go around the room and tell our dreams for the future. There were two rules for Dream Day: first, everybody had to share a dream. That dream could change from month to month (and they usually did), but no one was allowed to take a pass. And second, nobody was allowed to laugh at a classmate's dream, no matter how unlikely it sounded. Anybody who laughed, giggled, or so much as raised an eyebrow would have to stand out in the hall during the next month's Dream Day. Believe me, no one wanted to miss Dream Day.

I'll never forget Danny Raffield's dream. He was a lumbering, dangerous hulk, and not the sharpest knife in the drawer. The way I remember him, he was about thirty-seven the year we were both in fifth grade.

"So, Danny," Mrs. Burkett asked, "tell us about your dream."

"I want to be an astronaut," Danny said. He pronounced it "aster-nawt."

I didn't laugh (I had been warned!), but I did think, *Yeah, that's gonna happen. If Danny Raffield goes into space, it will be with the chimpanzees.*

Mrs. Burkett acted as if Danny's dream made perfect sense. She clasped her hands together and got this dreamy look as though she was looking into stars. She gushed, "Won't it be exciting for me when I'm sitting on my couch, watching television, and the news announcer says, 'There's Colonel Danny Raffield of NASA and the United States Air Force climbing into his space capsule … Wait, he's lifting the visor on his space helmet. It looks like he wants to make some kind of announcement.'

"And then imagine my surprise," Mrs. Burkett went on, "when you announce, 'I'd like to dedicate this flight to Mrs. Burkett and all the students of 5A.'"

Everybody in 5A erupted in cheers. "Hurray for Danny! Hurray for astronauts!" And I thought, *This imbecile is actually going to do it! Danny Raffield is going to fly to the moon.*

Maisey Blanchard was a pale, skinny little girl with crooked teeth and dishwater blonde hair that hung limp on either side of a sad face. She came from a poor family; she wore the same print dress to school every day, and her shoes were castoffs from her older brothers. Her dream, she said, was to be a movie star.

"Won't that be exciting?" Mrs. Burkett gasped. "I'll be settling into my seat at the movie theater with my Coke and my popcorn, and the lion will roar, and the screen will say, 'Starring Maisey Blanchard!' And I'll turn around and announce to everybody else in the theater, 'You might not realize this, but I taught Maisey Blanchard in the fifth grade.'"

Against all the evidence, I thought, *This girl is going to be rich and famous someday. I'd better be nice to her.*

"How about you, Mark?" Mrs. Burkett asked me. "What is your dream?" As far as I know, no adult had ever asked me that. I had never thought to ask myself. So I was as surprised as anybody when I announced that I wanted to write books when I grew up. Mrs. Burkett thought that was a brilliant idea.

I don't know if Danny ever signed on with NASA or if Maisey made it to Hollywood. But this is my fourteenth book, and I'm convinced I wouldn't have written the first word if Mrs. Burkett hadn't nurtured that dream. In fact, I might not have accomplished anything at all. I might not have considered what I really wanted to be or what I thought I was made to do. I might not ever have thought about how even my smallest dream could become a practical reality, about how dreams need plans and doing to take on earthly form. But all these things did happen, and they happened because someone looked at me as though I had meaning and asked what I wanted that meaning to be.

Now, with Mrs. Burkett's help, turnaround leadership becomes a simple thing to define: *it is a matter of asking the meaning—the dream—of an organization and doggedly executing a careful plan to make it so*. I first saw it modeled by a sweet, chubby woman who didn't even know how to pronounce *Mesopotamia*.

CHAPTER THREE

MY TURNAROUND LEADERSHIP JOURNEY

I first learned the art of leadership from a man named Dr. Paul Walker at a megachurch on the outskirts of Atlanta during the 1980s. By that time, I had completed graduate school and founded a small relief organization focused largely on projects in Africa. It was all going well, but I knew it was not everything I was made to do. So I had returned to the States to contemplate the next season of life. That was when the phone call came that still puts a knot in my stomach every time I think of it.

It was not my finest moment. The phone rang, I answered, and a deep, resonant voice said, "This is Paul Walker of Mount Paran Church." Dr. Paul Walker? *The* Dr. Paul Walker? The pastor of the ninth-largest church in America and the largest church in Atlanta? I laughed into the phone. I knew it was one of my idiot friends. "Paul Walker," I said. "Yeah, sure, and I'm Robert E. Lee."

Dr. Walker—for it actually *was* Dr. Walker—completely ignored my sarcasm. He was a serious man with a serious purpose. Thankfully, he didn't just hang up on me. He was calling to make a proposal. Mount Paran had two large locations eighteen miles apart and membership of more than nine thousand people. Dr. Walker had been shuttling between the two congregations on Sunday mornings, and it was wearing him down. He asked if I would be willing to come to Mount Paran for two years and help.

At first the idea seemed ridiculous. Talking to a village of curious Africans from the hood of a Land Rover was more my speed. What business did I have being on the staff of a high-profile megachurch on the affluent north side of Atlanta? It meant a change in how I had come to define myself, in what I expected from life. It was intimidating—but also exciting. Maybe it was indeed time for a change, time for an experience that raised my game. One of my great concerns was that I wasn't being challenged in what I was doing, that my work wasn't demanding more of me each day and forcing growth. Was Dr. Walker's offer a cruel distraction or the opportunity of a lifetime? After thought, prayer, and time spent reexamining our dreams, my wife and I came to see it as the latter and took the plunge.

Mount Paran was my graduate program in serious leadership. It was like the sun had come up on a new day. Everything I knew about leadership to that point I had acquired from graduate school and relief work in Africa and South America. But the sophisticated brand of multifaceted leadership required at such a large church? Nothing in my professional experience—indeed, nothing in my wildest imagination—had prepared me for it. Before I went to Mount Paran, I had assumed that leading a big organization would be like leading a small organization, only—well—bigger. I was in for a shock. Staff development, tactical planning, the innovative use of technology, sophisticated financial management, advanced administrative process—each of these was just a theory to me before that turning point in my life.

I would like to tell you that I stepped beside the esteemed Paul Walker and walked in leadership lockstep from that point on. It would be a lie. I didn't even know how to operate the phone system. I had never before had a full-time secretary. The thought of managing a secretary was more frightening to me than anything I had experienced in the Third World. There seemed to be no end to what I didn't know. A businessman friend once mentioned to me as an aside that Dr. Walker was "the best cash-flow man in Atlanta." I nodded sagely. Then, the first chance I got, I looked up the phrase *cash flow*. That's how clueless I was. Yet everything I learned made me hungry to know more. I remember thinking, *I want businessmen to talk about me that way. I want to be the kind of minister that businessmen respect professionally.*

I soon came to a crisis point. Clearly I had stepped in over my head. Maybe it was all a mistake. I envisioned myself running out my two-year contract, enjoying the ride, and then getting on with my life. I was forty-one years old—an old dog to be learning new tricks. Perhaps I should leave. But then I started to realize the opportunity I had been given to step to another level professionally. I looked at Dr. Walker and the men around him and said to myself, "I either need to improve my game to be able to hold my own with these men, or I need to get out." My hunger to grow outweighed my fear. I stayed.

I grew, but I made a lot of mistakes as I did. At Mount Paran I was like a guy who had been running a hardware store who suddenly found himself working side by side with Donald Trump. The first time I gave a speech as part of my new role, I mentioned to the audience that, having just come back from Africa, I had to go to Sears and Roebuck to buy myself some suits. Some folks actually laughed out loud. I had no idea why. I didn't know what I had said wrong. When I told Alison about it later, she gently said, "Mark, it's just Sears now, and I don't think anybody at Mount Paran is buying suits at Sears."

It got worse. The first time I sat on a stage with Dr. Walker, he leaned over and whispered, "Those shoes you're wearing—are they your best dress shoes?"

"They're my *only* dress shoes," I whispered back.

"Before next Sunday," he said, "get some new ones. If you can't afford them, I'll buy. But don't wear those shoes on this platform again." The lesson was clear. New stage, new shoes. Actually, new Mark Rutland. I wasn't in Africa anymore. I wasn't even just in Georgia. I was at Mount Paran, in Atlanta, at one of the most respected institutions in the country. It was time for what they call a *makeover*.

In his generous mentoring of me, Dr. Walker kept driving home the idea that a leader's self-presentation has to inspire confidence in those who follow. He insisted on professionalism. I had a doctorate but had never been called "Dr." Rutland. "You're not Mark here," Walker told me. "You're Dr. Rutland." It was never a matter of self-promotion. It was for the congregation's benefit, not mine, that he insisted that I be called Dr. Rutland. The congregation needed to know that it was safe to follow their leaders. Shoes and titles weren't the most important aspect of that confidence, but they were definitely a part of it. Dr. Walker was teaching me professional leadership in all of its facets. Mount Paran was a congregation of professionals who wanted their leaders to inspire confidence. Watching Dr. Walker at Mount Paran was one of the greatest learning experiences of my life. There I saw high-octane, high-energy, high-altitude leadership. I sat at Dr. Walker's elbow and saw genius firsthand. In short, he helped me step down from the hood of my Land Rover onto the platform of high-impact leadership.

I didn't learn turnaround leadership at Mount Paran, because Mount Paran didn't need turning around. What I did learn were the fundamentals of leadership and management. I learned financial management, budget preparation, and staff oversight. I saw how Dr. Walker worked with powerful people in the community on Friday and then how he encouraged a weeping woman after church on Sunday. I learned how to run a meeting. I saw business professionals ask Dr. Walker some hard questions, and I saw how he handled himself, how he let them disagree, how he compromised, and where he stood his ground. The give-and-take of business professionals was all new to me. I watched. I learned. I changed.

By the end of our original two-year agreement, I truly felt comfortable in Paul Walker's world. In fact, I came to love Mount Paran and all it taught me. I assumed I would stay there for years. Dr. Walker certainly wanted me to stay. He was always gracious. I felt, though, that I had learned what I had been sent there to learn. I had also begun getting phone calls about other jobs. Many of these appealed to me, and I took this as a sign that it was time for more. It was time for my first lessons in turnaround leadership to begin.

CALVARY CHURCH

The role I took next is best explained by describing one of my first meetings. Let me just say for the moment that I had agreed to become the senior pastor of a huge, troubled church. It was called Calvary Church. My first, revealing meeting after I took the lead wasn't with the board of deacons; it was with a roomful of officials from the bank that carried the note on our new auditorium. It was in fact this bank, not the church's board, that had dismissed the previous pastor. Now I had to go before them and give an account for myself.

We sat around a huge mahogany conference table on the top floor of one of downtown Orlando's tallest buildings—just me and nine men wearing suits that looked to be as expensive as my first car. If we began with pleasantries, I don't remember them. What I do remember is the man across the table who sat up very straight and said, rather unceremoniously, "Let's get one thing straight: you aren't the leader of this thing until we say you're the leader."

The borrower, as the ancient words go, is slave to the lender.

"I'm going to ask you a question," the banker said, "and I don't want you to hand me any spiritual nonsense."

Welcome to Orlando.

His eyes narrowed. "Can you turn this organization around?" It was the fifteen-million-dollar question. Could I turn it around? Could anybody turn it around? The financial issues were huge, but they were only symptoms of larger issues—organizational issues, trust issues, issues of culture and philosophy. The question was daunting, but I knew I had to answer in a way that would hide my queasy stomach and trembling hands.

"Well," I said, "I do believe I can turn it around. I have the experience. I have the background, and I think I know what to do. I'm also willing to work hard." I started to say that I believed God was with me, but, fearing the bankers would put that in the *spiritual nonsense* category, I refrained. "I believe I'm the man for this," I said simply.

The bankers looked at one another, clearly unconvinced. Anybody, I suppose, could sit there and declare himself to be up to the challenge of pulling a megachurch out of a death spiral.

"But as long as we're shooting straight," I said, "do you mind if I ask you some questions?"

The banker looked a little surprised. "Go ahead," he said.

"Here's what I'd like to know: who on your staff is going to get fired over this? You people must have been asleep at the wheel. Where does your bank get off loaning twenty-one million dollars to a failing organization? Now it's down to fifteen, and the bottom is out of the boat. The loan never should have been made. You loaned millions to an entity that's been hemorrhaging for a decade. Who authorized that?"

No answer.

I went on. "If you want our building, I'll give it to you now. There are twelve hundred people over there, and I'd be happy to take them elsewhere and start from scratch debt-free. If you tell me you want a unipurpose building in the suburbs with huge maintenance costs—if you think you know who you could sell it to—it's yours. But if you foreclose on me, I'm going directly to the *Orlando Sentinel* in twenty minutes and telling them that your bank forecloses on widows, orphans, and churches."

Things got very quiet in the boardroom. The bankers all looked toward the spokesman to see what he would say to that. He looked down at the back of his hands, clearly getting his thoughts together. Then a broad smile spread across his face, and he looked up and down the table at his colleagues. "Well, boys," he said, "we got ourselves a preacher who can talk business!"

That did it. I was in. I will always wonder if he had any idea how terrified I was. There was some bluffing in what I had said, but it worked—and it won me enough favor to let me get started.

Calvary was a unique and uniquely unhealthy congregation. Throughout the seventies it had been the crown jewel of the rising megachurches on the East Coast, but a sexual scandal led to nine straight years of decline. The congregation dwindled from nine thousand members to twelve hundred. In the midst of that death spiral, a kind of magical thinking took hold. The leaders got it into their heads that a building project would be just the act of faith to revive the church's moribund fortunes. I call it the *Field of Dreams* mentality—"If we build it, they will come." The church borrowed twenty-one million dollars to build a five-thousand-seat auditorium. Yet the *they* the leaders had hoped for didn't come.

Twelve hundred people is certainly not a small congregation. But twelve hundred people in a room built for five thousand—that looks like the funeral of a very unpopular man. Giving declined even faster than attendance, and it wasn't long before Calvary was upside down on the balance of that gargantuan mortgage. However, the financial and administrative problems were symptoms of deeper leadership problems. Taking on the pastorate of Calvary was a little like adopting twelve hundred abused children. Week after week I tried to communicate, "It's okay—Daddy's here." But if you had an abusive father, "Daddy's here" doesn't comfort you; it makes you flinch. For the first eighteen months of my tenure, Sunday mornings (not to mention staff meetings) were group therapy. I remember how thankful I was for the wisdom I had gained from the business-savvy atmosphere at Mount Paran. Thanks to that experience, I knew what questions to ask when I got to Calvary. The answers were devastating. It was a desperate situation, and it called for desperate measures.

Calvary's debt when I arrived was fifteen million dollars. Monthly debt service was $120,000. I went to weekly payments on the debt. I also scheduled a board meeting every Monday for a year. Since we were 120 days behind with our vendors, every Monday we counted the Sunday offering and then decided what bills to pay that week. Thankfully, offerings at Calvary surged well before we saw any significant increase in Sunday attendance. The reason was simple: once congregants began to see that we had a plan for dealing with our financial problems and that we were following through with the plan, they felt much better about giving their money. Previously, in the absence of real leadership, people had withheld their money. Who could blame them? They couldn't feel confident that their giving would do any good. Fortunately, as we started to demonstrate leadership, the offerings grew, and we were able to apply more and more cash toward that fifteen-million-dollar principal. The turnaround was in motion.

There was one thing I knew with certainty: the engine to drive any turnaround at a church is going to be Sunday morning. Whatever else we did, we had to get Sunday morning right. Church growth was not optional at Calvary. We had to have a hip on every seat in that huge auditorium and a wallet on every hip.

For years, even during its darkest times, Calvary had been the launching pad for every dog and pony show in the Christian world. I had never seen a church with more guest speakers and guest performers. Sunday after Sunday, authors with new books, singers with new albums, and every speaker with a variation on Christianity took the platform at Calvary to talk about their products and generate excitement. Some of the more cynical members called each week's oddity *Freak of the Week*. That was overstating, of course, but there was some truth to it. Weightlifters for Jesus, famous name singers, and people with wild testimonies attracted big audiences. Calvary had grown addicted to *the big show*. The problem was that those *guest stars* translated into little real growth for the church or for the people in the pews. It was all an illusion. With a star on stage, attendance seemed to surge. But the visitors who came for each big event forgot Calvary when the big event left town. And while they were there, they weren't especially likely to pull out their wallets.

During my time at Calvary, I preached 85 percent of the sermons. I spoke Sunday mornings, Sunday nights, and Wednesday evenings. I was determined to make Calvary's pulpit a place from which I articulated a vision for *Calvary*. I also wanted Calvary to be a place where people came to church the way people came to other churches—not for the *Freak of the Week*, but for community and truth and guidance. Week in and week out, I boiled that vision down to a simple, memorable message: "A Real Church for Real People Seeking a Real God." There had been a lot of hyper-mysticism and false spirituality at Calvary. It was time to get real. In other words, after a history of concealment and evasion, after decades in which the congregation didn't really know what was going on with its own church, we were going to be real with one another.

That consistent vision took hold, and the church grew. In the five years I was there, attendance tripled from twelve hundred to thirty-seven hundred. The chairman of the Orlando Chamber of Commerce described Calvary as the greatest financial miracle he had ever seen. The fact is that fixing the financial and administrative problems and growing the attendance were relatively easy. The deep cultural, emotional, and spiritual issues were much harder to address. Loyalty, trust, spiritual authority, and integrity had been squandered. Restoring those, not paying off millions in ill-advised debt, was the real leadership challenge at Calvary.

One of the most important things I learned at Calvary, my first turnaround, is that it's hard to know exactly what is going to work. Systems are complex, and so are people. At Mount Paran I filled my toolbox with tools, but how do you know which tool to pull out at a given time? That, of course, is what the rest of this book is about. But the short answer is that you make an educated guess as to which tools you need, you keep assessing whether your guess was right, and you keep making adjustments.

Calvary was like a Wild West town where the previous two sheriffs had been killed. Now there were bad guys and well-armed vigilantes, and one was about as dangerous as the other. The congregation's trust mechanism was badly damaged. At every announcement by the leaders, they reached for their guns. Dealing with this atmosphere of lawlessness required three main things. First, I had to be transparent.

The church had to know that what it saw of me was what it was getting from me.

Second, I had to be willing to make tough decisions with integrity and to stand by those decisions (in other words, be willing to pay the price of those decisions) no matter how loudly people screamed. The price, it turned out, was high. Unless you've lived through it, it is hard to predict the level of lawlessness and rebellion that exists in a leadership vacuum. When leadership makes a decision that some faction in the organization doesn't like, all hell breaks loose. It became apparent to me that if Calvary was ever going to become a unified body, a real church instead of a loose amalgamation of interest groups, discipline and firm leadership had to be restored. It was terribly costly at times. As I lanced the infections, toxic poison spilled out on me and on my family. Frankly, it hurt.

My third priority was holding loosely to my position and being open to leaving at any time. I am convinced you cannot effectively lead an organization that you cannot bear to leave. A determination to hold on, no matter what, will lead to a survivor mentality. And a survivor mentality is the diametric opposite of true leadership. A survivor does whatever it takes to survive, not to be a change agent, not to summon forth greatness in others. In the most difficult days at Calvary, I had to remind myself constantly that I did not ask for Calvary, didn't seek it, and therefore I could leave it when I felt led to leave.

After five years, when I felt it was time to leave, I left. The elders begged me to stay. They said it was wrong for Calvary for me to leave. More than one didn't believe I would actually leave. At a board meeting, a man asked, "How much more money do you want?"

I looked him hard in the face. "I've been with you for five years," I said. "Now, at the end, you're going to insult me? I'm not asking for money. I came because it was the right thing to do. I'm leaving because it is the right thing to do." And it was.

SOUTHEASTERN UNIVERSITY

After leaving Calvary, I spent three and a half relatively quiet years in Dalton, Georgia, managing the relief organization I had founded some years before. I traveled, I spoke around the country, and I healed with my family from the bruisings of leadership. I received many job offers, but none of those opportunities seemed right. After five strenuous years in Orlando, I wasn't in any hurry to return to the pulpit. Then I got a call from a small college in Lakeland, Florida—Southeastern College. Their president had recently resigned, and they wanted to know if I would be interested in filling that post.

I knew nothing about leading an educational institution. I had a doctorate, but I had never taught a single semester of higher education. The search committee understood all of that. They weren't calling me because of any educational expertise on my part. They were calling me because they knew I had led a turnaround at Calvary, sixty miles away and in the same denomination. Southeastern, they said, needed a turnaround of its own.

I already knew a little about Southeastern. It was a sad little campus situated at the edge of an alligator-infested lake. Enrollment had dwindled to nine hundred students, down from a high of twelve hundred fifty students some years earlier. A recent communication from the accountant had advised the board to start putting together an exit strategy. Southeastern, in short, was a tiny, shabby college on the precipice of collapse.

And yet Southeastern's interview process was the best I've ever seen. The board of directors simply offered the presidency to me. "Take it," they said. "Please take it." I did.

Then I began my initial evaluations of the problems. The CFO met me in the Atlanta airport for an interview. I asked the hard questions. With the school's finances in such disarray, I had assumed that the CFO was part of the problem. An hour of talking to him, though, showed me I was wrong. He didn't dodge a single question, and his answers were spot-on. "You seem to know all the answers," I said. "So why have things gone so wrong?"

The problem, the CFO explained, wasn't knowing the answers. The problem had been applying those answers. "I've never been allowed to do my job," he said.

There are plenty of people who say they want change but who aren't willing to pay the price. The leadership of Southeastern wanted to do what it took to turn its school around. The board was ready for change. They were desperate, and they didn't try to hide it from me. They didn't ask trivial questions, waste time, or demand that I fill out an application. They just said, "Will you do it?"

Surprising even myself, I took the job. It meant yet another new set of skills at the age of fifty-two. I knew leadership. I knew finances. I didn't know the world of education. Before I reported for duty in Lakeland, a friend sat down with me for hours and hours and taught me the basic nomenclature of higher education. This miniseminar helped me feel more capable and confident about leadership and staff management when I arrived on the campus as president in January 1999. I knew I could hire academics who could fill in the blanks on the educational side of things.

Frankly, my confidence started to wane immediately. The facilities were even worse than I had thought. Everything was run-down; there was mold everywhere. Every door, it seemed, was warped, and every ceiling seemed to sag. As for the landscaping—well, you could hardly call it landscaping. It varied from overgrown weeds to bare sand. Southeastern was an ugly little campus that looked like it might fall into the neighboring lake at any time. My vision for the place was bigger than buildings and grounds, but buildings and grounds were where our turnaround had to start.

A turnaround frequently requires that you show progress people can see. We had to get people busy with a successful first step to create a victorious culture and develop momentum. The imperfections of the campus were obvious to anyone. I had to get them to see possibilities. At Southeastern, a beautiful new dorm in the Mediterranean style was my goal. As soon as we could, we got started building the first half of that dorm. It generated a lot of excitement and hope for the future. I started giving visitors the most idiotic campus tours anyone has ever given. "And here is the spot where three twenty-million-dollar buildings are *going* to go.... Over here is where the gym *will be*...."

While faculty, staff, parents, and prospective students were hearing this speech over and over again, I was working sixteen-hour days on the less glamorous but more vital aspects of the turnaround. At Calvary, Sunday morning services had been the engine of the turnaround. At Southeastern, I realized, the engine had to be the admissions department.

What had been known as the admissions office at Southeastern was actually just the registrar. The school didn't do much recruiting. It mainly waited for its own denominational families throughout the South to drag their freshmen to campus. Southeastern became grade thirteen for that denomination's high school kids.

As soon as I could, I changed the name of the so-called admissions office to *Registrar*. Furthermore, I moved admissions under the CFO, who had an MBA with an emphasis in marketing, and he seemed perfect to guide a new admissions department. When I hired a young man from a larger college to direct admissions, we basically handed him a phone and said, "Build an admissions department—from scratch."

"How do I do that?" he asked.

I shrugged. "That's for you to figure out."

"But where are my prospects? What about a database?" he asked.

I shrugged again. "We don't have any. You'll have to figure that out too."

"Oh, by the way," I added, "that half dorm we're borrowing money to build … you need to fill that up, or you and I both are going to be fired."

Early on in my Southeastern career, I gave a speech on *selling the invisible*. We couldn't sell nice buildings; we didn't have any. We couldn't really sell the excellence of our academics, much of which was substandard when I got there. We could sell two things: leadership and vision. We promised to make leaders of our students. We became a *Leaderversity*—a term coined by leadership guru Ken Blanchard when he first visited the campus.

We started getting some momentum. One building project led to another. We were able to hire some excellent faculty members, who raised the expectations for our entire faculty. In the ten years I was at Southeastern, 85 percent of the faculty turned over. I released a few faculty members, but not many. Most of those 85 percent were professors who chose to quit rather than step up to a new level.

Vision was the key to everything. I could hear Mrs. Burkett whispering in my ear. I started referring to Southeastern College as *the University*, though we hadn't made any official change. The first week I was on the campus we registered the name *Southeastern University* with the Florida secretary of state. I was casting a vision, and people caught it. One professor told me, "This is the first time I feel like I teach at a real college. I have always felt like a counselor at a summer camp."

Momentum grew. We borrowed to pay for that first half dorm, but the increased revenue from more students allowed us to build a second dorm, then a third. Then we renovated the old dorms. Then we built a new gym. Then a swimming pool. We converted the old gym into an intramural center, built a student center, and renovated the chapel. A gorgeous restaurant followed, then a new business building. In the ten years I was at Southeastern, we completed thirteen major building projects totaling almost sixty million dollars. We transformed the campus into a gem of Mediterranean architecture. The student body grew from nine hundred to more than three thousand during that time period, even as we raised tuition.

ORAL ROBERTS UNIVERSITY

At the end of ten years, Southeastern was humming. I was over sixty and ready to dial down. I was just beginning to think that I would spend the rest of my life at Southeastern when the phone started ringing. The calls were from a very persistent headhunter. He was only doing his job, I guess, and what a job it was: to find a new president for Oral Roberts University in Tulsa, Oklahoma.

ORU was in desperate need of a turnaround. Oral Roberts, who had built the university into one of the country's most important Christian institutions of higher learning, handed the reins over to his son in 1993. Things did not go well after that. Years of decline reached a point of crisis in 2007, when three former faculty members sued the school for unlawful termination. The mismanagement that came to light in the process further tarnished the university's already blemished reputation—beyond repair, some observers believed. Everyone from the IRS to the regional accrediting body was watching ORU as the grim news mounted. This scrutiny put ORU in the glaring headlights of an oncoming locomotive called *scandal and bankruptcy*. The school was fifty-five million dollars in debt, and most of that was consumer debt rather than mortgage debt. The deferred maintenance for the old buildings added up to another fifty-five million. Under overwhelming pressure, Richard Roberts resigned in November 2007. Unfortunately, all this played out in the national media and was broadcast around the world. The expected collapse of ORU was front-page news.

In short, ORU was a train wreck—until the miracle happened. David Green of Oklahoma City, the owner of the Hobby Lobby chain of craft supply stores, announced that his family was willing to give ORU seventy million dollars as long as the school met certain conditions that he and his son, Mart, worked out. Those conditions included a total change of leadership and a move to what the Greens called *twenty-first-century governance*.

That was where I came in. The headhunter was calling me to be the first outsider to lead ORU. My first reaction was to laugh. I had read about ORU in the paper, and the thought of leaving my comfortable situation in Florida for such a monumental undertaking seemed ludicrous. The more I thought about my comfortable life at Southeastern, though, the more my comfort there seemed like a reason to leave rather than a reason to stay. The machine was running itself at Southeastern; the college had millions in the bank, and after a lifetime of refusing to play it safe the thought of playing it safe now felt a little like dying before I was dead.

My wife, Alison, came around before I did. She saw that ORU was the right move for us. Several dear friends also weighed in and encouraged me to make the change. There was much to consider. An important factor for me was my respect for Oral Roberts. I didn't want to see his legacy die. I also didn't want my comfort zone to dictate my destiny. Then again, my age was a big concern. If you fail at age forty, you have plenty of runway left. But at age sixty, I had to face the possibility of an otherwise successful career ending in a spectacular failure. In time, though, I knew: I was going to ORU.

I knew one thing from the start and communicated to the ORU board: I wasn't at ORU to be a legacy president. I was there as an out-of-town gunslinger. I could come in and clean up, but I couldn't stay there and run things. I could be the marshal, but I couldn't be the mayor. My job was to clean up the mess, build up momentum, turn the school around, and get ORU ready for the next phase of its journey.

When I arrived at my office on the seventh floor of ORU's magnificent Learning Resource Center, I found something very peculiar.

The elevators stopped on the sixth floor. You had to have a key to get to the seventh floor, where the president's office was. Even the stairwell doors were locked. I had no idea that this was how things had been for decades at ORU—the president and his inner circle sequestered away from everybody else. "This makes no sense," I said to my executive assistant. "How is anybody supposed to get up here? Get the elevator unlocked. Unlock the stairwell doors."

That very afternoon, the head of security was in my office. "Dr. Rutland, I just got word that you wanted the seventh floor opened up." He eyed me warily. "I'm not going to do that until I hear it straight from you."

"All right, then," I said. "I want the seventh floor opened up. I want the elevator unlocked, and I want the stairwell doors unlocked."

The head of security tilted his head back and squinted at me. "You're sure about that?" He was genuinely concerned, and his serious tone was causing me to doubt myself.

"Well, now I'm not as sure as I was. Is there something I don't know?"

He shrugged. "It's just that occasionally we get some real loonies on this campus."

"Oh, good heavens," I said. "Just unlock the doors!"

Nothing else I have done at ORU has created the kind of on-campus sensation as when I unlocked the seventh floor of the Learning Resource Center. Students rode the elevator to the top floor just to look around. They texted their friends. They called parents and alumni to say, "You're not going to believe where I'm standing!"

I was sitting at my desk in what was once Oral Roberts's office when I heard a faint knock on my open door. I looked up to see an older faculty member standing at the threshold. "I teach here," he said.

"Come on in," I said.

"Oh no, I don't have to come in," he said, as if such a thing were unthinkable. "I've been at this university for forty years, and I've never seen this office."

"Well, come on in," I repeated. He stepped through the door sideways, as if to take up as little space as possible. "Have a seat," I said, directing him to the sofa. "Tell me about your career here." I was moved by my time with this man, and it was obviously a healing moment for him. It seemed that the whole ORU family was healing along with him.

I had no way of knowing how significant the rather obvious gesture of unlocking the seventh floor would be. Everybody on campus understood that at ORU the elevator now went all the way to the top, both literally and figuratively. Once a fortress of mystery, a place shrouded in secrecy, the seventh floor of the Learning Resource Center was suddenly a symbol of a new openness. The great irony of ORU's culture before I came was that it was so tightly controlled in terms of governance by presidential fiat—the closed seventh floor being the symbol of that control—while being utterly out of control in terms of finances, morale, public relations, and a dozen other areas. My task was to tighten up the controls in most areas while loosening access to my own office and otherwise creating a looser, lighter atmosphere.

My motto became "Open up, lighten up, loosen up." We got serious about making ORU "the most joyful campus in this or any parallel universe," as I told the students every week—and it worked.

I quickly saw one engine capable of helping drive the turnaround at ORU. It was chapel, which met twice a week. I spoke at almost every chapel—something that is virtually unheard of among other college presidents. I had to get my message of joy and affirmation out to the students and faculty, and chapel was the one opportunity to have them all assembled so I could pound my message home.

I was fortunate to find a faculty at ORU that was surprisingly whole and healthy. I had no idea what to expect from them. There had been tremendous tension between the faculty and the previous president, even to the point of lawsuits. For all I knew, the faculty would be permanently embittered and hostile. Only three years earlier, Harvard's faculty had run President Larry Summers out on a rail. I knew I might be joining him. As it turned out, the faculty was more than ready to embrace the changes that I brought. As I reached out to the faculty members, they reached out to me. Shared governance between faculty and administration was one of the conditions of the Green family's bailout of the university, so the faculty was highly motivated to play an important role in the turnaround. It didn't hurt that ORU's faculty had been world-class from the university's earliest years.

At Southeastern, we had built a university more or less from scratch. ORU was a very different thing. ORU was a great university that had forgotten it was a great university. It was my job to remind faculty, staff, students, and alumni what a great organization they were a part of. We had to find ways to signal that it was a new day at ORU.

The Green family's millions were a huge luxury. Instead of working our way out of a deep hole as we had done at Calvary, or trying to build as we did at Southeastern, the worst of the financial crisis was over by the time I got there. The buildings needed repair, but at least they were built. Enrollment started up, and ORU began to move. Soon, we were operating in the black. Freshman retention rate in my first two years was over 80 percent, up from 72 percent in 2009.

More important was that ORU was no longer a sad, depressed, joyless, angry place. I came onto campus not just as president, but also as Chief Culture Officer. I pushed joy every day. Abraham Lincoln said that it was the job of the commander in chief, after a victory or after a defeat, to walk among the troops. I walk up and down the aisles in chapel. I eat in the cafeteria when I can. I hug students and let them know that they matter to the university and to me. I go to meetings and joke with the faculty members. In short, I tell them that they are great people at a great place. The wonderful thing is, it's true.

"All shall be well, and all shall be well, and all manner of things shall be well." That, I suppose, is the most important message of the turnaround leader. You sound the all clear: there are no more bombs in the building; everybody's safe now. You announce that there's new management. Then you articulate a new vision—a happier vision.

At Calvary, at Southeastern, and at ORU, I often thought of Churchill, alone behind that BBC microphone during World War II, speaking a bigger reality to his people as the Nazis menaced from across the Channel in a fallen France: "Let us therefore brace ourselves to our duties, and so bear ourselves that if the British Empire and its Commonwealth should last for a thousand years, men will still say,

'This was their Finest Hour.'"[1] This is the great art of turnaround leadership. The leader steps into an organization in its darkest hour and says, "Friends, you only *thought* this was your darkest hour. In fact, this is your greatest opportunity. Let me show you why that's true."

CHAPTER FOUR

BEFORE THE NUTS AND BOLTS: LEADERSHIP AS AN ART

We have more leadership consultants and experts than ever in our world—and less true leadership. Perhaps this is because leadership is easy to describe but much harder to do. Leadership may be the one arena where that old, insulting maxim is actually true: "Those who can't, teach." Yet if a man who can't lead teaches leadership, you get impractical ideas and abstractions rather than mandates for action. This concerns me. I'm about training leaders. Untested leadership theory just gets in the way—the artificial drives out the genuine.

One of the reasons you can't learn everything you need to know about leadership from a seminar or a book is that leadership is, ultimately, an art. I know this may sound mystical and maybe out of reach, but it is absolutely true. A sculptor knows his next move by an inner sense rather than by an objective measurement. A musician can play a piece of music with technical skill, but she hasn't become a master until she has an inner connection to what she plays. Leadership has an intuitive aspect too. Science helps you lead. Statistics and research help you lead. Medicine and psychology help you lead. In the final analysis, it may well be the way a leader has developed his art—sharpened his leadership senses and fine-tuned his leader's intuition—that will ultimately prevail.

This is why, before we consider the nuts and bolts of the leadership engine and perhaps before you even step on the property of the institution you have to reinvent, I want to describe a few elements of the art.

It has been said that leadership is about doing the right things; management is about doing things right. While I understand the distinction that is being made in that statement, I see it otherwise. Leadership and management are simply two essential parts of true servanthood in legitimate authority. Servant-leadership comprehends visioning with a group of people—as the leader, yes, but with a servant's heart. Servant-management is about the practical empowerment of that vision, yet still with a servant's heart.

When leadership and management collide, it is *not* because one or the other is wrong; it is because true servanthood has been lost in the balance. When leaders lose their sense of servanthood, they yield to hubris, resist wise counsel, refuse to listen, and run past practical managers who are truly trying to make the vision work. When that happens, train wrecks follow.

When managers, especially middle managers, lose their sense of servanthood, they become bureaucratic bullies. Rules and regulations in their hands are not the rails the vision runs on but the wall it runs into. They lose track of the fact that management functions exist to empower others, not themselves. When that happens, the trains stop moving.

When servanthood surrenders to narcissism and arrogance, rules trump vision, and regulations are more important than people. Leaders who forget they are servants drive into walls. Managers who forget they are servants set booby traps and then gloat when others fall in. The issue is not so much whether leadership is more important than management. The issue is that without the great lubricant of servanthood, the gears will grind until they grind to a halt.

Leadership is Eisenhower essentially saying, "We're going to liberate France and move toward Germany by the summer of 1945." He was leading the service of liberty. Management then had to make it work. Management was making sure there were enough tanks and troop carriers and food for the GIs. Management was figuring out which roads were passable and making sure that once the trucks and tanks were on the road, they didn't outrun the supply line. Management is the practical execution of the vision. The managers who made Eisenhower's vision happen were servants of the vision.

Leadership and management exist together only in the spirit of servanthood. Serving the people we lead is a challenge because, admit it, people are weird. They are unruly, fuzzy at the edges, contradictory, and, well, strange. This means that while scientific analysis will help you move ten million units from Tokyo to Los Angeles, the people who do the moving cannot be made better by science alone. They need fully engaged leaders who know their art.

Broadly speaking, leadership is visionary while management is about logistics. Leaders and managers are both vital to the success of an organization. Servant-leaders need servant-managers, and vice versa. The extent to which they sometimes drive one another crazy is in inverse proportion to their comprehension of servanthood. The manager's tendency to see things in black-and-white is an important check on the leader's exuberance. A good servant-management team, one that listens, that pays attention to detail but resists the impulse to hinder action, is a great luxury to a high-flying visionary leader as long as he will listen. The servant-leader has to be able to hear the truth. He has to communicate that he wants to hear the truth—indeed, that he demands the truth. Managers have to understand that their job is not to stop the vision or even slow it; their job is to make the vision happen.

Never forget what Winston Churchill said: "We want a lot of engineers in the modern world, but we do not want a world of engineers."[1] He meant that while we are thankful planes fly, our microwaves work, and our cell phones do their miraculous duty—all the gifts of engineers—we don't tie an organization to a vision through engineering alone. We need leaders who have a feel of the human situation, who have developed a *people sense* that allows them to coach, inspire, cajole, comfort, and perceive the human dynamic. In short, a leader has to be an artist of the human spirit.

People often speak of *building* a company or an organization. The building metaphor suggests structures that hold things in place. It speaks of stability and solidity. It is a comforting metaphor: you work hard to put up walls, and there those walls stand, holding everything in, holding everything together. A place for everything and everything in its place. But when it comes to a turnaround, the idea of a building, with its rigid structures, is not the most helpful metaphor.

When leading a turnaround, the central concept isn't the building of structures (though you will certainly be doing plenty of that) but the managing of tensions. By tensions, I don't necessarily mean stress in a negative sense. Our very bodies are held together by tension—the tension of muscle against muscle, muscle against bone. It's tension that makes it possible for us to move. Without tension, you'd just be a puddle on the floor.

So instead of the metaphor of *building* an organization, imagine a room, the sidewalls of which are electromagnets—perfectly balanced and equally powerful electromagnets. Theoretically, if you were to throw a handful of iron filings into the geographical center of the room, they would dart around in the air until, ultimately, they found an equilibrium at which they would be suspended in the air by tension between the magnets pulling at them from either side.

A similar equilibrium is what gives shape to a healthy organization. If somebody opens a door in our imaginary magnetized room, or if the air-conditioning comes on, the draft or the change in air pressure will make the iron filings move. Everything will be in flux until the filings find their equilibrium again. Maybe one of the electromagnets loses some power. There will be another shift.

In an organization, it's not rigid walls that hold things in place. Rather, it is ever-shifting forces, pulling and pushing until things begin to find equilibrium. The electromagnet pulling from one side of your organization is chaos. The electromagnet pulling from the other side is control. Chaos is movement, heat, energy, just as the movement of molecules in a body is heat and energy. Zero degrees Kelvin—absolute zero, as it's called—is the point at which molecular movement in a body has stopped. Without chaos, there is no life. But ultimate molecular chaos—chaos with no control—is nuclear fusion. In an organization, chaos is where creativity, freedom, and energy happen. It is also where all the train wrecks happen.

Put in leadership terms, chaos is where high-octane leaders and entrepreneurs live. Control, on the other hand, is where the accountants and lawyers live. Neither is a bad thing. Control is the home of the procedures and policies that keep the wheels from flying completely off. It's no coincidence that the words *policy* and *police* look so much alike. Policies, like the police, keep things from getting out of control. Policies prevent the train wrecks that are inevitable in chaos. Indeed, in the case of ultimate control, there are no train wrecks because none of the trains are moving. If the danger of chaos is train wrecks, the danger of control is paralysis. The answer to both dangers is servanthood.

Twenty-first-century leadership is all about understanding where your organization is and where it needs to be on the chaos-control continuum. It's a moving target. If total chaos is a one and total control is a ten, the ideal point of balance isn't necessarily a five. It varies according to where your organization is in its life cycle. The infancy of an organization, like the infancy of a person, is all chaos: demand at one end and a problem at the other. There is no order, no schedule. Adolescence is much the same. So is an organizational turnaround. You have to allow for more chaos than you would in a better-established organization.

In the prime of an organization, you are negotiating the tension between chaos and control, trying to hit somewhere around a five. Another way to talk about it is the tension between speed to market (chaos) and accounting (control). The chaos mongers in the marketing department are pushing you to get next year's model out the door to beat the competitors to the punch, product recalls not withstanding. The accountants and lawyers are putting spreadsheets in front of your nose, showing how much a recall is going to cost you if it comes to that.

Or you have a crack salesman selling a thousand computers a month, but he won't turn in his expense reports. And when he does turn in the expense reports, half the time he doesn't turn in any receipts. The CFO, Mr. Control, hates the guy and comes to you, insisting that you do something about it. You're saying, "A thousand computers a month!"

The CFO is saying, "Sure, but I can't find the money."

You say, "He says it's coming."

"But it's not here ... and furthermore, he's turning in expense reports without receipts." That salesman, the son of chaos, is like a cow a friend once told me about. She gave far more milk than any other cow, but she put her nasty hoof in every third bucket.

At some point you have to decide how long you're willing to live with the ongoing train wreck in order to sell a thousand computers a month. Do you say, "I'd rather have three guys selling three hundred and thirty each and turning in their expense accounts"? Or do you tell the CFO, "Figure out the expense account. Work it out. Don't call me. Don't call him. Those thousand computers pay your salary every month. He sells a thousand computers. You sell nothing. Do the math"?

I'll say it again: in all organizations, the leader is ever on a continuum between chaos and control. One of the skills—it's an art, really—that a leader must master is the almost inner sense that the organization needs either more chaos or more control. There is no science to this. There is no objective measurement. We have to know our people, know our corporate culture, and know the goals we've set out to achieve. If we begin to fear chaos and tighten down the controls too much, we'll have order but no creativity and, well, no life. A cemetery should come to mind. But turn completely toward chaos, and a riot results. The corporate culture will feel like static electricity—excited and even fun, but unproductive.

The valves for your organization are over at the control end of the chaos-control continuum. But the steam that actually powers the machine comes from the chaos end of things. You can't have one without the other. That's the tension of the chaos-control continuum.

That equilibrium moves, and a leader has to be flexible. I don't mean a leader vacillates or is indecisive; I mean a twenty-first-century leader is willing to move and respond according to changing circumstances. You have to discern what is happening around you, both inside and outside your organization. You have to nudge things one way or another. This is the art of the leader.

Keep in mind that I'm talking about a tweak here and there, not sudden, radical changes. There is an ancient proverb that says, "Avoid changeable people." Indeed, wild, erratic swings in leadership numb followership. If you're always making big changes, your followers learn that *this too shall pass*. They learn to keep their heads down. No matter what the leader announces, nobody gets on board. Instead of inspiring people, that kind of leader deadens them.

At the opposite extreme is the rigid leader who refuses to change at all. I don't know much about auto racing, but I do know that the driver who plans his strategy and rigidly refuses to change speed or direction is liable to get himself killed and to kill others. Only a fool would lock his wheels against the infield rail and say, "I'm an inside driver; that's what I do. I'm going to stay against this rail the whole race, come hell or high water." Inside driving may be a great strategy. But if you're not willing to pay attention to flags, listen to your pit crew, negotiate around obstacles, and take into account every change in context, you're far more likely to die than to win.

Every leader has to steer a course between radical changeability and inflexibility. A leader has to be able to see when the organization needs a shift. If you're going to show this kind of flexibility in your methods, you have to have a great deal of confidence in yourself, your team, and your mission. There are plenty of people who mistake rigidity for conviction and who equate flexibility with moral compromise. The greater your sense of selfhood in leadership, the more comfortable you will be with flexibility. And if you negotiate this well, you *will* be criticized by those who are rigid.

There are times when, in dealing with errant employees, an intuitive leader will need to say, "I realize that this isn't who you really are; we can work with you to straighten this out." But there are other times when the offense will seem much the same, or even less egregious, and the intuitive leader will say, "I'm sorry, but I can't deal with that. You can't remain in this organization." There's no exact formula for knowing which approach is appropriate in a given situation—when to lean toward *management* and when to lean toward *leadership*, when to lean toward *liberty* and when to lean toward *structure*. Sometimes you just have to trust that you see the big picture better than anybody else and that you know which tweaks to make. But you're going to have to educate your staff and your board to stay with you in the process. They need to know that you're not always going to do everything in the same way at the same speed every time.

In physics, Heisenberg's uncertainty principle states that you can measure a particle's position or you can measure its velocity, but you can't reliably measure position and velocity at the same time. The same is true in an organization. That's why it takes a certain amount of intuition. You have to feel your way through.

You no doubt have your own preferences and prejudices regarding chaos and control. If your style is managerial, you will be more comfortable at the control end of the continuum. If your style is more entrepreneurial, you will be more comfortable at the chaos end of the continuum. If your comfort level lies toward chaos, any move toward control will feel like imprisonment. For the control-minded, any step toward chaos will feel like moral compromise. You've experienced this phenomenon when you drive on the interstate. No matter what speed you're driving, anybody who's driving five miles an hour slower than you is an idiot, and anybody who's driving five miles an hour faster than you is a crazy person.

Because I tend to be more comfortable closer to the chaos end of things, I struggle most with the control freaks in my organization. Yet I know they are necessary. Even if you as a leader can somehow manage to live permanently on the chaos end of the scale, your organization certainly can't. The wheels will fly off eventually. On the other hand, if you yield entirely to the police at the control end of the continuum, your organization is headed toward decline. The guardians of the flame—and by this I mean the guardians of conformity and control—will have taken over. The sound you hear will be innovation and change breathing their last.

Now here is how we apply this leadership art. If you have come to your organization from the outside in order to effect a turnaround, pay particular attention to the organization's history immediately prior to your arrival. On the one hand, that history will tell you whether you need to move things toward chaos or toward control. On the other hand, that history will determine how far you can move the organization and how quickly. There are two questions here: where should we be, and how close can I get to that spot, given the history that these people are reacting against?

In the three turnarounds I have led, two were complete disasters when I got there and one was a situation that had swung from chaos well past the point of balance over to control. I can't say it is easy to tighten up from chaos toward balance, but you don't encounter nearly the resistance you do when trying to pry open the hand of control and loosen things up. There were still bodies strewed all over the tracks when I arrived at Calvary in Orlando. It wasn't hard to convince people that we needed to write policies and implement procedures and calm things down. People didn't always like the techniques I used to implement balance there, but nobody denied that the institution needed more financial balance, operational balance, staff balance, and theological balance.

ORU, on the other hand, had gotten a new board just before I came along, which recognized that things were totally out of control and tightened the screws. By the time I got there, part of the wreckage had been cleared away, and some of the bodies were buried. On the chaos-control continuum, however, they had gone straight from a two to a ten. The fear of the past and its excesses moved the new leadership to an uptight control mechanism that had a hair trigger. It wasn't all just a board issue either. Control is always an effort to deal with fear, and the ORU I found was wounded and fearful.

Some alumni even wanted to control everything from who led worship in chapel to how much money was spent on the smallest items. And I initially made things worse. In my effort to put the accounting house in order (an absolutely necessary step), I gave accounting too much power. That caused a chaos-control tension I never fully resolved. Indeed, it is not fully resolvable anywhere in any organization, as far as I can tell.

When I got to ORU, the passionate desire for control and order had replaced the chaos of the past, but joy was the unintended victim. The tension was palpable, but at least nobody's hair was on fire. It was easy enough for me to see that they desperately needed to lighten up and loosen up—to move from a ten to something more in the five or six range. But the resistance from the existing corporate culture was strong. Any time I challenged this entrenched control, I was taking a significant risk. It looked like I was trying to return things to the bad old days before the new board had taken over. People looked askance at my efforts to nudge things back toward balance. If you're trying to move an organization away from excessive control, you have to take it slowly and constantly explain your vision and your purpose for every move. This is the only way to set people at ease and get them on board.

These were people who still remembered the gruesome sight of the catastrophe that was ORU in the '90s and the first decade of the 2000s. When the paralysis is absolute, it's hard to move off the control end of the continuum. The attitude at ORU when I arrived was, "If we just follow the policies more thoroughly, everything will work right." So though they needed to loosen up, they kept tightening up. They couldn't see that things were grinding to a halt for lack of energy. A slow death by paralysis isn't nearly as gruesome as a train wreck. But death is death.

There are two kinds of folks in every organization—control freaks and freewheelers. I should point out that if you are leading a complex organization, your job might be complicated by the fact that not all parts of the organization are at the same place on the chaos-control continuum. When I first arrived at ORU, the one area of the organization that needed more control than any other was finance. In that department, the freewheeling damage was still being done. I replaced almost everybody over there.

There was a shortage of policies, best practices were ignored, and accounting was a mess. And as I said, I initially overreacted. In an effort to bring order out of chaos, I let the policy mongers nearly grind everything to a halt. As a result, there was constant tension between the chaos-oriented entrepreneurs and the control freaks. Sometimes the tension was healthy; sometimes it was not. There were times when I had to grit my teeth and clamp down on the chaos, which is not natural for me. There were also times I had to say to the control freaks on the staff and the board, "Can we lighten up a little? Are there any times when the forms don't have to be filled out completely? Has there ever been an exception? How do we work exceptions?"

Sometimes I felt like I was coming into the emergency room where there was a big sign over the triage nurse's desk: "You must show insurance card before receiving treatment."

"But are there exceptions? What about if there's an open wound and blood is pouring out? Do you have to show your card then, or is that an exception?"

"That's an exception."

"Good. Let's write that one down. Now, are there any other exceptions …?" Eventually you start to nudge things toward a place where the need for creativity and intuition and energy is in balance with the need for control.

At Southeastern University the control mechanisms were totally different. Overcontrol at ORU was the fully understandable over-reaction to a crisis of chaos. The control at Southeastern was rust; the gears were rusted shut. At ORU the wheels had flown off from fast, wild driving. At Southeastern the wheels hadn't moved in so long they were frozen. At ORU debt had nearly sunk the place. At Southeastern we had to lubricate frozen gears and wheels to get the thing moving. At ORU debt had to be paid off. At Southeastern we had to acquire enough debt to dislodge the dust of death.

Modern medicine tends to get postsurgery patients up and moving faster than in the past. Southeastern wasn't in a crisis of chaos. The problem was that it had sat there so long, gangrene had set in. The risk of speed to market is always a risk of introducing too much chaos too fast, but at SEU, death was at the door. Waiting was not an option.

The point is that flexible leadership along the control-chaos continuum depends upon context and history. You cannot raise every child the same way. Furthermore, you cannot parent a child the same way at every stage of his life. In the same way, you cannot lead one organization at the same level of chaos or control as you might another organization. Good leaders move nimbly on the continuum, ever in sensitive response to historical changes in their organization. They understand that every organization is unique and that every season of every organization is unique. You have to fine-tune along the control-chaos continuum constantly to get the balance right. It is one of the great arts of turnaround leadership.

In the old movie *The African Queen*, the riverboat captain, Humphrey Bogart's character, jumps up every now and then in the middle of a conversation and kicks the engine or hits it with a hammer. He has heard some sputter or cough in the engine that nobody else even notices, and he gives it just the little adjustment it needs to correct itself. Creative, intuitive executive leadership is like that. Everybody else thinks things are purring along, and the leader senses something that needs adjusting. He springs into action, tweaking this, nudging that. It's art as well as science.

When I came to ORU, my initial systems analysis told me that the amount of financial aid we gave was too high. We were giving away so much that it felt to me like we were buying customers at the expense of our financial health. What kind of school uses tuition as a loss leader? So I told the admissions and finance departments that I wanted to dial back the discount rate, or the amount of financial aid.

Surprisingly, we grew anyway, but slowly. So the next year I asked admissions and the finance department to raise the discount rate again. But the original message had stuck. "We thought you said you wanted to lower the amount of financial aid," they said.

"Right," I answered. "That is what I said last year because that's what we needed last year. This year, we need more customers." Truth to tell, I don't really have an opinion about what the discount rate for a university ought to be. I have only a control panel. And sometimes we move the dial this way, and sometimes we move the dial that way, according to what our organization needs at the moment. The boat motor makes a noise, and I smack it with a wrench; it makes another noise, and I give it a kick. But I don't necessarily know what I'm going to do to it an hour from now. The twenty-first-century flex leader must figure it out. Once he knows his role as servant, he can begin to tinker with dials. Creativity and flexibility combined with a servant's sensitivity make a powerful alloy for meaningful change.

PART II

THE SEVEN STEPS OF THE TURNAROUND

CHAPTER FIVE

STEP 1: FACING INSTITUTIONAL REALITY

Before Interstate 75 was built, drivers traveling to Florida went right through the middle of Corbin, Kentucky, on Highway 25. Every day hundreds of them stopped at Harland Sanders Café for a bite of Colonel Harlan Sanders's fried chicken. But when the interstate was complete, Highway 25 went quiet, and Sanders Café was left high and dry. Colonel Sanders was at a crossroads. He could hope for the best and ride his near-empty restaurant all the way down, or he could pursue another vision for his restaurant.

Colonel Sanders's fortune grew out of the disaster that ensued when I-75 bypassed his hometown. He hit the road and started recruiting Kentucky Fried Chicken franchisees across the United States. It all began with a clear-eyed look at a situation that had changed completely. That willingness to face reality is not as common as it should be among leaders.

There's an old joke about a Southerner in a bar who was going on and on about the superiority of the Confederate army. The South had better generals, he said, and more fighting spirit, and they were better shots than the Northern soldiers. "The South could have beaten the North with cornstalks," he concluded.

A nearby patron, growing impatient with the loquacious Southerner, asked, "Then why didn't the South win the Civil War?"

"Because the North wouldn't use cornstalks!" the Southerner answered.

As this joke suggests, the Confederacy's greatest problem in the Civil War was a tragic refusal to face its reality. The South rushed into a war against a vastly superior force in large part because it believed its own PR.

True, the Confederacy had the great generals. True, Southerners had plenty of fight and home field advantage, if you can call it that. In their own minds at least, they had a cause they believed in. But none of that changed the fact that the North had well over twice the population and nine times the manufacturing capacity. No amount of generalship or fighting spirit was going to outweigh that kind of advantage in manpower, horsepower, steel, and iron.

The leaders of the Confederacy were not alone. In dysfunctional organizations, very few leaders are willing to face the reality of their situations, and it often leads them from disaster to disaster. Companies say they are on the cutting edge—maybe even believe they're on the cutting edge—when they haven't changed in years or, in any case, haven't changed nearly as much as everybody else around them has changed. They don't take the time to really drill down into the facts. The highway has bypassed them, and they won't face it.

THE IMPORTANCE OF SEEING

The first step in leading a turnaround in an organization is simply to take a good long look at the stark realities—and then to communicate those realities to everyone involved in a way that avoids panic. In many ways, faith-based organizations are the worst about refusing to face reality. To face such earthbound realities as financial trouble, and to take them seriously, is sometimes construed as a lack of faith. Earlier I mentioned that Calvary Church took on twenty-one million dollars in debt in large part because of what I call *magical thinking*. The leaders there believed they were trusting God when they took on huge debt even while their revenue was dwindling. Common sense, in their way of thinking, would have been a kind of spiritual compromise, a lack of faith. They may have thought they were submitting their decision-making process to God. In fact, they were surrendering their decision-making power to the bank.

In one of my first meetings with the Calvary congregation, not long after my meeting with the bankers, I conducted an exercise in transparency. At a church-wide business meeting, I turned down the lights in the auditorium and put the church's financial reports on the overhead projector. As we went through PowerPoint slide after PowerPoint slide, the situation became obvious. I had just gotten into the darkest numbers when somebody yelled, "My God, we're bankrupt!" That sucked the oxygen out of the room.

Disruptive, yes. But it was also a big help. The whole point of the meeting was actually to alarm the people of Calvary, to wake them up to their situation. After sleeping through years of crisis, they awoke to the shouts of their fellow congregant.

I managed to get things calmed down enough to continue the meeting. "I'm glad you're awake," I said. "But now isn't the time to panic. That time would have been months ago, maybe years ago. Now, instead of panicking, we're going to turn this thing around."

Why are leaders so reluctant to share distressing news with the people they lead? I have already mentioned the faulty theology that often keeps leaders from addressing facts. There is also the reality that people prefer the happy illusion, however short-lived, that things aren't really that bad. And there is always the fear of what people will say or think or do when they find out what is really going on. This is not always an unfounded fear, by the way. People do sometimes freak out, overreact, shoot the messenger, and otherwise make life unpleasant for bearers of bad news. But that unpleasantness is nothing compared to the unpleasantness that ensues when the ship hits the rocks.

After years of denial and concealment, the simple act of showing those shocking financials to the congregation turned out to be one of the most important things I did as I went to work on Calvary's turn-around. For one thing, people knew what was at stake. But perhaps more importantly, the vague sense that something big was wrong was replaced by a concrete sense of just how bad things were. Yes, it was a huge financial mountain to climb. But it was *finite*. It was something we could start chipping away at. It gave us a reason to roll up our sleeves and start working together instead of just chewing our fingernails, waiting for the other shoe to drop.

The revelations of our congregational meeting were followed by incremental and very tangible actions. We were 120 days behind on our bills, so I went to Florida Power and appealed to them to leave our lights on. I told them, "If you'll wait, we'll pay you everything. If you shut off our power, you won't get anything." In our Monday morning board meetings, as we reviewed the previous day's offering, we decided together which bills to pay next—and we met our financial obligations week by week until we had caught up with all the overdue bills.

It was amazing how quickly the congregation stepped up once it understood the reality of the situation. One of the scariest things we uncovered was the fact that three hundred and fifty thousand dollars in designated missions funds were on the books, but the money wasn't there. Realizing the urgency, we called upon a small inner group of people to give, and because a new confidence was starting to permeate the congregation, we were able to put that three hundred and fifty thousand dollars back almost immediately. Within the first six months, we saw a six hundred thousand dollar cash turnaround.

Chipping away at those money troubles was not the solution to all of Calvary's dysfunction. Nevertheless, being aware of the magnitude of their financial problem had a curiously invigorating effect on the people. It gave them something to work toward together.

THE INSTITUTIONAL POSITIVES

I should also point out that being aware of institutional realities means more than revealing an organization's weaknesses. It's also a matter of seeing and understanding the organization's strengths and assets. I'm a big believer in top-line management: that is to say, all things being equal, I would rather improve the balance sheet by growing top-line assets than by cutting bottom-line expenses. And getting more out of existing assets is usually a much more efficient means of improving the top line than acquiring or creating new assets.

At one point I actually considered titling this chapter "First, You Need a Billionaire." The turnaround at ORU would probably not have happened without the munificent intervention of David Green and his family. We will never know, of course, from what other direction God might considerably have brought rescue, but David Green was such a miraculous answer that another seems unlikely.

It would be easy for ORU to be smug, to say, "Well, the answer to a financial challenge is a billionaire, and we got one. And you don't have one, and nonny nonny boo boo." It would likewise be easy for others without a billionaire popping out of the woodwork to fall to paralyzed despair.

The point, however, is not really some miraculous *deus ex machina* like David Green. As grateful as we are and as grateful as anyone is for a generous donor, you cannot wait for that. The point is to take advantage of whatever resources you have at hand to start the turn.

Calvary's asset was also its problem. The facility was fabulous. Visitors came just to see it. The facility, however, caused the debt and much of the anger. The debt and the anger were easy to see and feel. Less apparent were the benefits. I didn't have to build anything. Neither did I have to limit growth. Room, I had. Plenty of room.

A neglected asset is like found gold. Looking through old records at Calvary, I also noticed that the church had hours and hours of prepaid airtime with a local television station. A previous pastor had decided that he wasn't suited for television, so those credits were just sitting there, unused.

I called the station and said I was ready to start broadcasting Calvary's services. Through a series of events I won't detail here, we ended up airing four times a week without having to pay a cent. In subsequent years, Calvary went through a period of tremendous growth. Our research showed that 33 percent of the people who joined our church during that period were first exposed to Calvary through those television broadcasts. It was a result of paying careful attention to the whole of our institutional reality, both the good and the bad.

In the systems-analysis phase of a turnaround, look for what you *do* have. Anyone can see the challenges. A visionary leader must see the opportunities and creative ways to leverage resources.

At Southeastern College (as it was named when I went there) it was easy to see the pathetic decrepitude. But what I saw was a blank canvas. The buildings and grounds were so bad, no one, absolutely no one, I thought, would *protect* them from improvement.

It turned out I was wrong about that. There were actually a few who dug their heels in to guard the status quo, even as horrible as it was. But they were few, and the *new*, all-new campus at Southeastern was possible *because* the old one was so horrible, not despite it.

As Paul Newman told George Kennedy in *Cool Hand Luke*, "Sometimes nothin' can be a pretty cool hand."[1]

UNDERSTANDING YOUR INSTITUTION'S WORLDVIEW

In order to help your organization see its institutional reality, it is important that you understand the worldview through which your organization interprets (or fails to interpret) all facts. There are as many organizational worldviews as there are organizations, but I group them into three main categories: history-oriented views, location-oriented views, and vision-oriented views.

A historical worldview will typically be dominated by one of two historical mythologies or a combination thereof: the Golden Era or the wounded past.

Happy memories of a Golden Era—a time before the current regime was in place—would seem to be a good and positive thing. On the contrary, such memories, whether they are accurate or not, make things very hard for a turnaround leader. Your goal as a turn-around leader is to turn the organization around to success. But your constituents aren't necessarily looking for you to lead the organization to success; they may be looking for you to lead the organization back to its golden age. Not a recipe for success.

On the other hand, an organization with a *wounded past* historical view might see everything you do through the lens of past hurts. Competing against those phantom pains is even more difficult than competing against the golden age. If anybody has ever ripped off your constituents or deceived them or humiliated them or disappointed them, you are suddenly the receptacle for all those feelings.

I was visiting a church once—just visiting—and an agitated-looking guy stopped me in the hall and said, "I hate that tie."

I said, "You do? I don't know what to say to that. Should I have called you this morning and asked what tie you would like me to wear?"

He answered, "The former pastor here used to wear a red tie and black suit just like you have on, and when I see that red tie, all I can see is him standing up there in that pulpit." That was a bad case of an emotional-historical view of things. My tie triggered bad emotions from a wounded history.

Take it from me—it is a difficult moment. I have already described my experience in Orlando. I took over a church that was emotionally, psychologically, spiritually, and financially bankrupt. I was not paid for the first six months. We were 120 days behind on our bills. I stood in the pulpit that first Sunday and gave the congregants a big smile, and to them it looked like I was baring my teeth—another big, bad wolf. Whatever I tried to do, my board members viewed it from the perspective of their wounding, and it created suspicion: *what are you trying to pull? What is this all about? We weren't born yesterday, you know.*

Another possibility—and this isn't so very unusual—is a view that combines Golden-Era thinking with the wounded past. It's the worst of two worlds. "We've been victims these last few years, but what makes it worse is the fact that things were so exciting in the Golden Era that came before that." Now you're measured against the benevolent giant of the distant past while being held responsible for the depredations of the recent past. And, of course, the recent past probably wasn't as bad as they remember, and the golden age wasn't as great as they remember. In either case, your best hope of breaking through those historical prejudices is to show integrity, be consistent, and tell the truth over and over again—until you are sick of hearing it.

There is also the location-oriented worldview. In the chaos-control discussion earlier in this book, I mentioned the fact that you can measure location or you can measure velocity, but you can't measure both at the same time with similar accuracy. You may find yourself in the middle of an organization—and particularly the board of an organization—that is fascinated with measuring the exact location of your organization, judging things based on where you are *right now*. There are people in your organization whose whole job is to assess current location—accountants, for instance, and lawyers and HR professionals, people who are responsible for creating a snapshot of where the organization stands with regard to financial, legal, and other measurable realities. Those people are vitally important. But a snapshot isn't a vision.

If you have a board that is location-obsessed, it can encrust your organization with policies and procedures like barnacles on a ship. They want to police everything. Audits and legal issues can grind you to a halt. A location-oriented board can become highly obstructionist. They aren't opposed to success; they are opposed to change. They want success in terms that are measurable right this minute. That is what they measure first. I keep mentioning the board in this context because it is not a problem for, say, your head accountant to be location oriented in her view of things. That's her job. It is a problem, however, when the people who are in charge of making decisions for your organization can't assess velocity or direction because they are so concerned with current location.

The location-oriented board might say, for instance, "We don't owe anybody anything! We're debt-free! Debt-free!" Freedom from debt can be a great thing. But it can also be a self-limiting factor. There is good debt, and there is bad debt. The location-oriented board, insisting on measuring success right here and right now, loves cash on hand. "We're debt-free, and we have a million dollars in the bank!" So they hold everything right there. That million dollars feels so good, they don't want to drain it down by investing in the future. "You say the company needs a new truck? That would draw our cash down to $970,000. No can do."

The third worldview is that of the vision-oriented organization. This is what you want, of course. This organization sees the vision, the purpose. They are on board with you. It is not the employees' or members' job to set vision. That is your job. Their job is to take steps to implement that vision. A truly holistic visionary view takes into account the history of the organization, the rules and policies, the people, and the vision. Ideally, the people in your organization grasp the vision of where you are headed without sacrificing people or ethics to the vision. It is only in this visionary context that the people in your organization will truly be able to see the reality of their situation.

RESPECTING THE PAST, ENVISIONING THE FUTURE, SEEING THE CURRENT REALITY

ORU is a *nameplate* university. The O and R stand for something. I had to know what that was. I knew Oral Roberts. He was there at my inauguration as president. He gave his blessing to a Rutland presidency. I took that very seriously.

One thing I have learned about leadership is that when things go well, the leader gets more credit than he deserves, and that when things go poorly, the leader gets more blame than he deserves; it's just another failure of institutional reality. At ORU, I had to negotiate that for my own tenure, but that negotiation was complicated by the credit and blame borne by my predecessors at that institution.

When people said, "That's not the way Oral did it," I had to say, "No, that's not the way Oral did it … in 1964." I loved the man. I felt great loyalty to him. But that doesn't mean that I needed to make all the boys wear suits and ties and make all the girls wear skirts the way Oral did in the '60s.

So, on the one hand, I had some legalistic, angry, old alumni saying, "If you just made all the boys wear ties, ORU would look like the place Oral Roberts had in mind." But on the other hand, I had younger but equally angry alumni saying, "When you do this or that, it looks like something that happened in the bad time."

I had to negotiate all that and figure out a way to bring ORU's culture to a place where it could accept and embrace its past, affirm the good parts, acknowledge the troubled waters, and move into a fresh vision. That is hard work, and a leader may have to spend a lot of political capital to make it happen. That is part of the reason that the turnaround leader isn't usually the legacy leader for an organization. It may take all he has to put the institution in a place where the legacy leader can take over. The turnaround guy is a gunslinger. He comes in, runs off all the bad guys, cleans up the saloons, then gets on his horse and rides off. You don't hire a gunslinger to be the mayor.

One thing I knew about my time at ORU: I wasn't creating a Golden Era. I was creating a tidy-up era. I was getting the university's culture to a place where there was internal joy—heat, light, movement, growth—and getting everything in order so that a legacy president could come in and not have to do a cleanup. Part of seeing my institutional reality, in other words, was seeing that my best service to that place was necessarily short-term service.

A SPECTACULAR FAILURE TO SEE INSTITUTIONAL REALITY

Thus far, our discussion of institutional reality has worked from the assumption that you, the leader, have a clearer view of reality than the people you are leading, and that the reality check goes from leader to follower. I want to close this chapter with a cautionary tale that shows how important it is for you to create and sustain a culture in which your followers feel free to give you a reality check when you need it.

Early in the seventeenth century, England, Spain, Holland, and even tiny Portugal had established themselves as major naval powers. But Sweden was not among the great powers on the sea. They had some of the single-deck ships that were typically found on the Baltic but none of the great men-of-war that prowled the oceans. And even in the limited arena of the Baltic, the Swedish navy was nothing special, having suffered several defeats at the hands of the Polish navy and just as many defeats at the hands of bad weather in the 1620s.

King Gustav Adolphus decided it was time he established Sweden as a major naval power. He had enjoyed a great deal of military and geopolitical success in his first decade on the Swedish throne. In 1626 he commissioned a warship that would be perhaps the greatest ship of his era and certainly the most magnificent vessel in the Swedish navy. It was to be named the *Vasa*.

King Gustav Adolphus's ego demanded that the ship be the biggest, the best armed, and, above all, the most beautiful. He added great statues and other heavy ornamentation to the *Vasa*. Worse, he added a second deck of extremely heavy guns. The result was a top-heavy vessel. Gustav Adolphus may have been a good king, but he was a terrible engineer. The ballast, which would have been sufficient for the original design, was no match for the weight that had been added above the waterline.

When the *Vasa* was nearing completion, a Swedish admiral began to have serious doubts about her seaworthiness. He did a *run test*, in which thirty sailors on the top deck ran from one gunwale to the other to test the stability of the ship. After only three trips back and forth, the ship was rocking so violently that the admiral halted the test for fear that the ship would capsize right there in the shipyard.

The structural problems could be fixed. The keel could be deepened, and more ballast could be added to account for the above-water changes. But that would mean a significant delay in the ship's launch. And the king had made it clear that he was in a hurry to get the *Vasa* on the seas. The Thirty Years' War had been raging for ten years; believing that his new ship was a game-changer, he wanted it in the fray as soon as possible.

Even though it was obvious that the *Vasa* was a disaster waiting to happen, nobody had the courage to tell the king. He was out of the country anyway and not very accessible, though he did send frequent letters expressing the urgency with which he desired to see the great *Vasa* on the open sea.

On August 10, the *Vasa* launched, right on schedule. King Gustav Adolphus was still out of the country, but a large crowd, including ambassadors from a number of European countries, came to see the great ship launched. With much fanfare, the *Vasa* left the slip and sailed out into Stockholm Harbor. The sailors and passengers—some of them families of the ship's officers—waved from the deck. It was a pleasant day with a slight breeze. The ship had not yet traveled a nautical mile when a slight gust of wind caught the sails. That one gust pushed the *Vasa* dangerously toward its port side. The sailors scrambled, and the ship managed to right itself, but no sooner was it upright again than a second gust knocked it over again. Water rushed in at the open gun ports. Within minutes, Sweden's great naval hope was a hundred feet below the surface of Stockholm Harbor. More than thirty people died.[2] All because King Adolphus created a negative atmosphere drenched in such ego that no one dared tell him the bad news.

If your subordinates don't feel free to tell you bad news, you will suffer for it. Gustav Adolphus no doubt thought of himself as communicating well in the weeks prior to the *Vasa* disaster. He sent a number of communiqués expressing his wishes. But he had created a culture in which no one could shoot straight with him about the realities of his situation.

Create a culture in which your subordinates are able to say to you, "You are going to sink this company." If you can't hear that, you are in trouble. That doesn't mean you have to do everything that your subordinates tell you to do. You're still the Decider, as George

W. Bush used to say. You are free to say, "I hear you, but I still think I'm right in this situation. And if it turns out I'm wrong, I'll be the first to admit it."

In 1961, marine archaeologists raised the *Vasa* from the bottom of the harbor. Since 1988, it has been housed in its own museum, one of the most popular tourist attractions in Stockholm and a monument to the dangers of poor leadership.

CHAPTER SIX

STEP 2: COMMUNICATING A VISION

You've met the kind of person who simply radiates vision: the coach who strides into a locker room and tells the team members on a long losing streak that he sees them going to the Final Four—and makes them see it too; the techno-geek whose passion for a new kind of computing makes the rest of us see a different kind of future; the moviemaker who redefines the way we go to the movies. Here is what each of these knows: real vision casting changes the way people think and see and feel.

That kind of vision and leadership isn't simply something that you're born with or not born with. You have it in you; the key is letting it out. Many leaders are afraid to let their visions radiate.

They're afraid of disappointment later. They're afraid of radiating the wrong vision. And those are risks, I suppose. I believe that those are risks worth taking.

It doesn't take all that much skill or leadership or management insight to come into a hard situation and see what's wrong. Real visionary leadership is about coming into a situation and saying, "I see something here that isn't immediately obvious. I see big things, good things. These obvious problems aren't the whole story. They aren't even the main story."

It certainly didn't take a genius to see that Southeastern College was falling apart when I got there. I have already mentioned the mold and the water damage and the general disrepair and the work-farm architecture of the place. But it didn't take me long to realize that this wasn't just a shabby, run-down campus. It was a blank canvas. One of the great things about those hideously ugly buildings was that nobody was particularly attached to them. This campus could be whatever we wanted it to be. We could do something beautiful there.

In Italy my wife and I had seen a beautiful hotel with the light stone walls and tile roofs that are so common around the Mediterranean. It occurred to me how well that architecture would suit sun-drenched central Florida. It took some imagination to picture that grand hotel where those sad, dark buildings stood. But I had just enough imagination to see it.

I took two members of Southeastern's executive team out to an empty field on campus crisscrossed by narrow dirt tracks where students cut across from the dorms to the classroom buildings. "Let's talk about what's going to go right here," I told them. "Picture a big, beautiful fountain, the kind of thing you'd see in a square in Rome, with pillars all the way around. And there, picture a big statue." In Texas I had seen a statue of Jesus washing the disciples' feet, and it seemed like just the kind of thing we needed. "Now, forget about those little dirt bunny trails cutting across the field. Imagine wide sidewalks where thousands of students can walk back and forth across the quad, which will be surrounded by buildings in the Mediterranean style."

The executives stared openmouthed. Mediterranean style? Fountains? Thousands of students? They looked like they were trying to decide whether I had received a vision from God or had just dropped acid. This was a little Bible college tucked away in Lakeland, Florida. This wasn't how things were done around there.

Eventually those two men and the rest of the leadership team started to catch the vision. I imagined Southeastern as a great cruise ship that had backed onto a reef. We had to nudge the thing off the reef and sell tickets at the same time—lots of them, lots more than a mere nine hundred of them—to get the ship off the reef. We had to sell the invisible, to borrow the title of one of my favorite management books. "This way to the cruise," I was saying. "Just look at that wide beautiful sea out there. Reef? What reef? And never mind those men at the pumps ..."

Before long we were actually building. The first modest start was a mere half dorm. But over the course of ten years, we completed thirteen major building projects, raised what we could, financed the rest, and completely transformed the campus into that Mediterranean style we envisioned, standing in that empty field. By the end of that decade, more than three thousand students were walking on our transformed field of realized dreams.

Even the most convincing visionaries don't convince everybody, though. Some people just aren't going to make the trip with you. That's okay too. The sooner they get off the bus, the better. When the first half dorm was complete, I asked all the faculty to walk with me up a little hill where we could clearly see both the new dorm and the legacy campus. I pointed at the new dorm gleaming in the sun. "That's where we're headed," I said. "That's the future of Southeastern." Then I pointed at the old campus. "And that's the past. That's over. We're leaving it behind. If you're there," I said, "you can't come here with me. And I need for you to tell me. Because we're moving on."

That afternoon, two faculty members came to my office and offered their resignations. They were concerned that putting so much emphasis on facilities would destroy the spiritual life of the campus. "Let me get this straight," I asked. "You're saying that living on a shabby, run-down campus makes our students more spiritual, and living on a beautiful campus will somehow make them sinful?" It wasn't that, they said. It was a matter of emphasis.

This is an important point: it is okay if people leave because they don't share your vision. I disagreed with those professors, but I appreciated their honesty, and I appreciated their integrity in saying, "No, I just don't see things the way you see them." They might have feigned enthusiasm and secretly tried to undermine the things I was doing. Instead, they told the truth and chose to go rather than be dragged along toward a vision they could not share.

A SPOONFUL OF VISION MAKES THE MEDICINE GO DOWN

Vision touches everything you do in your organization. It was vision that made it possible for the faculty at Southeastern to push through the hard, frustrating process of watching massive construction projects appear all over campus while they were woefully underpaid.

There was no doubt about it; it was disgraceful to see what the faculty members were making when I arrived at Southeastern. They deserved better pay; furthermore, I understood that there could be no sustainable turnaround for that school unless they were paid fairly. But the institution was hanging by a thread financially. They had been robbing Peter to pay Paul for decades, and the deferred maintenance was staggering. The physical plant was a wreck. The school charged surprisingly low tuition at that time, but that had resulted in a campus with such a low-rent look that nobody would dream of paying higher tuition to attend there. The perceived value was spiraling downward.

I had some difficult choices to make. I desperately wanted to raise the faculty's salaries, but I had to have more financial margin before I could do that. And to get that financial margin, I had to invest in the buildings. I needed to raise the perceived value of Southeastern College so I could raise the tuition so I could have the margin I needed to raise faculty salaries. I need to point out here that setting priorities is not necessarily a matter of asking what you value most. It is a matter of asking what is strategic. I value professors more than I value buildings. If I was going to invest in buildings before I invested in faculty salaries, the faculty deserved an explanation.

I called a meeting with the entire faculty. I showed them a table of faculty salaries for the Southern region of the Coalition of Christian Colleges and Universities. Southeastern ranked right at the bottom. "Listen," I told them, "it's disgraceful how poorly you're paid. I realize that. Nevertheless, this institution doesn't have the money to raise your salaries." There were groans all around. They had heard this before. "However," I said, "I can get the money." This was something new. "As soon as I get the money, you're going to get a raise. I promise you that. But I need you to wait, patiently. I need you to be patient when you see me building new dorms. I need you to be patient when you see me spending money on landscaping. It's hard to watch somebody build a fountain when you're barely making enough to live on. If you will wait and be patient, the cavalry is coming."

I communicated a four-step process to the faculty:

1. Fix the facilities.
2. Recruit more customers who are willing to pay a higher price because the perceived value was increasing.
3. Create margin.
4. Raise faculty salaries.

I couldn't raise salaries without margin, and I couldn't create margin without improving the facilities. I've talked to thousands of high school seniors in the middle of the college decision process. They ask about the dorm they're going to live in. They ask about the student center. They ask about the exercise facilities and the sporting events. Sometimes they ask about classroom and lab facilities. I have never once had a prospective student ask whether the faculty is paid fairly. As for donors, it's easier to find a wealthy alum willing to pay for a fountain with his name on it than to find somebody to donate money to raise faculty salaries.

The faculty members held their noses and watched as we launched a campaign and poured money into the facilities at Southeastern. They continued to eat Ramen noodles while we built a beautiful new dormitory. When the dormitory was built, we filled it up, which created a little margin.

That little margin financed a tiny raise for the faculty. I met with them again. "See that dorm?" I said. "It paid for that raise. It was a tiny raise. I understand that. But I need you to hang in there. We're making progress, just as I told you." Most of the margin generated by the first dorm went not to faculty salaries, but to a second dorm. But some went to salaries. When that second dorm was built and filled, the faculty got another incremental raise. We hopscotched from building to building, raising salaries incrementally as we went.

At last we reached a point where the growth in perceived value at Southeastern allowed us to start raising tuition. More students paying higher tuition meant significant financial margin. When I left Southeastern in 2009, we had the highest-paid faculty in the Southern region of the Coalition of Christian Colleges and Universities.

We had to have a comprehensive strategy to get there. We were guided by a long-term vision and a strategic plan. If resources were unlimited, priorities can always immediately reflect values. But resources are always finite. We have to make hard choices that sometimes appear in the short run to conflict with our own stated values.

That can be a tough message to a professor who is watching buildings go up while she still isn't getting a fair salary. I rehearsed the plan constantly. "I know this feels like it's taking a long time. Hang in there. Help is coming. We're making progress. The plan is working." Executives who anchor change in their organizations are those who talk the most clearly and persuasively about vision and about where the culture of the company is headed. A good strategy becomes a bad idea when kept a secret.

You cannot overcommunicate your vision for your organization. Everyone in your organization needs to be able to articulate the vision. That will happen only if you communicate it until you are sick of hearing it come out of your own mouth—but you keep communicating it anyway. When you have communicated the vision to everybody you know, you're just getting started.

One of the amazing things about the leadership of Oral Roberts was his ability to communicate a vision. He summed up his vision for Oral Roberts University in five words: "Go into every man's world." Oral Roberts University's whole reason for existing is to raise up people who hear God's voice and are prepared to go out into the wider world and make a difference. In an evangelical milieu that tended to emphasize separating from the *ungodly*, Oral Roberts saw it differently, insisting that the students of ORU be prepared to go into every world—the business world, the communications world, the arts world—and win the admiration of their peers in order to bring glory to God. He resisted anything that would marginalize Christianity in the larger culture—especially ignorance. That vision drove real excellence on ORU's campus. When I arrived at ORU in 2009, I was amazed at the fact that seemingly everybody on that campus—from the tenured professor to the first-semester freshman—was able recite that vision: "Go into every man's world." ORU presented its share of challenges, but that shared vision was one of the great assets that I had to work with when I arrived.

In my effort to communicate a fresh vision, I proclaimed ORU to be "the most joyful campus in this or any parallel universe." I pound away at it every time I address the students. But I apply this principle to smaller matters, too. When I instituted a missions offering in chapel, you can be sure every student at ORU knew what our goal was: one hundred thousand dollars. I repeated it over and over again, and we repeated it together. It is not possible to overarticulate vision. As a matter of fact the ORU students and faculty have exceeded one hundred thousand dollars in giving to foreign missions every year since. And they applaud every time the plate is passed!

VISION AND ORGANIZATIONAL STRUCTURE

You've seen *vision* statements that were obviously the result of perfunctory exercises. It's vision by committee. Nobody will ever pay attention to those things. They're a waste of time. True vision shapes everything about an organization. So often you see an organization that is basically a feudal system; there is a one big king who rules over a bunch of little rulers, each with his own little fiefdom to rule and territory to protect. Nobody is pulling in the same direction. Organizational feudalism is a failure of vision casting on the part of the leader. The productive model is what I call a comprehensive model. In the comprehensive model, everybody knows the vision of the house because the organizational leader is pounding away at it, repeating it, teaching it. That leader is making sure that every tributary within the organization is feeding into the confluence that is the vision of the house. Everything that happens in the organization emanates from a core value, a central vision.

It is no easy task to move from a feudal model of organization to a comprehensive model. If your subordinates are accustomed to ruling and protecting their own little fiefdoms, they won't be eager to let them go, no matter how miserable the feudal system has made them. But if you are going to be a turnaround leader, you are going to have to make this transition.

One of the most impressively comprehensive organizations I have ever been exposed to is the Indianapolis Colts. I interviewed Tony Dungy for a magazine shortly after their Super Bowl victory. I took my son and two grandsons with me. When we got to the entrance, the security guard greeted us with an enthusiastic "Welcome to the headquarters of the World Champion Indianapolis Colts. How can I make your day better?" When we entered the building, the receptionist said the same thing: "Welcome to the headquarters of the World Champion Indianapolis Colts. How can I make your day better?" When we got to Coach Dungy's office, his secretary greeted us the same way. Everybody was on message.

After we had waited in the reception area a few minutes, an assistant came out of Coach Dungy's office and said, "Coach asked me to apologize and let you know that he is going to be about ten minutes late. They're in there picking out Super Bowl rings." Ten minutes? Can I tell you how often my dentist or doctor has made me wait half an hour without any explanation? And Coach Dungy is apologizing for making me wait ten minutes? While he picks out Super Bowl rings with multimillionaire superstars?

When Coach Dungy came out of his office, he greeted my son, grandsons, and me as if we were old friends. He gave the boys Colts souvenirs and talked to them as if they were the most fascinating people he had ever met. He gave me the interview I wanted as if nothing was on his mind except answering my questions. Then the PR man took over and gave us a tour of the building. As we walked past helmets of every team in the NFL, one of my grandsons noted that the Philadelphia Eagles helmet was missing. "That's right," said the PR man. "Good observation. We don't have their helmet up yet." And to congratulate my grandson for being so observant, he gave him a Colts hat. I've attended churches that are not as joyful as the Indianapolis Colts organization. The culture of the Colts organization permeated everything. Everything fit together. They were giving us the same message at every level, in every medium. They made Colts fans out of us all.

THERE'S NO SUCH THING AS OVERSTATING VISION

In fascinating slow-motion photography, Dr. Mike Wheatland, a professor at the University of Sydney specializing in solar astrophysics, demonstrated the quite surprising movement of a suspended Slinky. Holding the Slinky at the top, he let it hang straight down, *unfurled* as it were. He then let go. The slow-motion photography proved that for a time (brief though it was) the bottom end did not fall. The Slinky collapsed from the top down. The sections at the top began to contract while the bottom stayed where it was.

This was caused, he explained, because the *information* that the Slinky was no longer held in place at the top took some period of time to reach the bottom. In fact, by the time that *information* did reach the bottom it was distorted. The very top sections of the Slinky contracted straight down, but those nearer the bottom eventually began to twist. The implications for leadership are huge. Leadership is communication.

> 1. Information from the top never gets to everyone at every level at the same speed. The faster and *purer* it does, the less of the message gets twisted.
>
> 2. Organizations do not collapse *up*. They collapse downward. Failure of leadership at the executive level doesn't immediately reach the mailroom. But it will!
>
> 3. The collapse is not immediately apparent from the outside. To the naked eye the dropped Slinky seems to be suspended in midair. When leadership loses its grip at the top, it may take a long while or a split second for the whole thing to fall, but during that interlude everything may actually give the appearance of holding steady.

At the risk of being repetitive, I'm going to finish this chapter with this reminder: when it comes to articulating a vision, you cannot get bored with the sound of your own voice; it doesn't matter that you've said it a thousand times. That doesn't mean your audience has heard it—really heard it—a thousand times. The vision gets fractured, scattered, and twisted as it goes down through the ranks. It loses power and focus. You have to gather all those pieces up and speak them again with fresh energy. Speak the vision with enthusiasm and vitality every time, as if it's the most fascinating thing you've ever said. If you show the slightest boredom with your own message, that boredom will be more contagious than the Ebola virus.

Communicating vision to your organization is the one responsibility that you must not delegate. Your subordinates need to hear the message directly from you, their leader and help. Even if there's somebody who is a more gifted communicator than you, resist the temptation to let that person commandeer communicating the vision. The organization follows the person who articulates the vision. If you let somebody else do that, you're asking for serious disloyalty down the road. The people in your organization must know the vision and echo the vision, but the voice they echo must be yours.

CHAPTER SEVEN

STEP 3: ALIGNING MARKET, MESSAGE, AND MEDIUM

When I was in Africa, I was astonished at how much weight Africans could carry on their heads. Slender women and even children could carry heavy water pots or huge piles of sticks or bundles of laundry the size of a pony—burdens that I couldn't carry ten yards—and walk for miles. Their secret is alignment. We Westerners carry loads out in front of us or to the side or on our backs. But by carrying loads on their heads, Africans bring the burden into alignment with the strength of their skeletons. Alignment is crucial to strength and health.

Alignment is vitally important for an organization, too. The organizational equivalent of skeletal alignment is the alignment between market, message, and medium. If you get those three things in alignment, you will be amazed at the heavy lifting that your organization can accomplish. Any organization, whether it is in turnaround mode or not, needs this kind of alignment. I focus on it here because if your organization is in need of a turnaround, it is a sure bet that your market, message, and medium are out of alignment. You have to line them up before you can hope to turn your organization around.

UNDERSTANDING YOUR MARKET

It is a Texas truism that if you shoot into a covey of quail you aren't likely to hit a single quail. If you want to shoot a quail, you have to aim at a quail. If you have a shoe store, to whom are you going to sell shoes? The answer isn't *everybody who needs shoes*. You won't hit a quail if you aim at such a big covey. Be specific. You're selling shoes to the well-heeled college male, or to people with foot pain, or to nurses and other people who are on their feet all day and need comfortable work shoes.

When I came to Calvary Church, I had to think long and hard about who, exactly, our market was. Being in Orlando created some unique challenges when it came to defining our market. Orlando is a strange place. We had the faith healer Benny Hinn a few miles to the north; we had Mickey Mouse a few miles to the south. And yet, like any city, Orlando was full of people who were looking for something authentic and solid. In a town known for great shows and slick production values, we realized that our market was considerably more *real world* than Disney World. Our market, we realized, was all those people who longed for a Spirit-filled church experience but were put off by spiritual excesses and the hyperdramatic spectacles. Not to put too fine a point on it, our audience was the people whose theology was more charismatic than Baptist but who had ended up at one of Orlando's many Baptist churches because they weren't comfortable with many of Orlando's Charismatic churches. Even in the church market—especially in the church market—segmentation is a key first step in understanding what business you're even in.

Market segmentation and specialization require a certain amount of courage. By choosing to focus on one segment of the market, you are choosing not to focus on other segments to the same extent. You can't be afraid to let those people go elsewhere. In other words, the segment you choose to hit with all your energy becomes your target. There are many segments of the market; one of them is your primary market.

One of the most challenging tasks of the leader is to identify the right target for the right time. How? There are three factors that must be considered.

1. *Size*: Is this a niche market so small that it cannot sustain your operation? Furthermore, is the size of the market shrinking? The World War II generation is a segment of the market, a valued and revered segment. They are also passing from the scene at the rate of a thousand a day.

2. *Productivity or Profitability*: Can the target you identify be made to produce (energy, resources, and so forth) at a high-enough rate to even pay the bills?

Choose a big market with no resources, and the size may be impressive and the results disastrous.

3. *Reachability*: Do you have or can you achieve access to this target? You may choose a target that is large and potentially lucrative but is equally impossible for you to reach. Not all media reach all markets the same. How will you communicate brand benefits to the target market?

Having said all that, remember there are also *touching* targets. In other words, if you choose target B, targets A and C are close by. The law of proximity is a powerful determinant of success. Choose widely scattered and highly disparate targets that don't *touch*, and suffer for it.

Suppose your target is young Latino families in a certain area of the city. You are far more likely to also reach their grandparents than other young families from the mostly Anglo neighborhood across town. This seems obvious, doesn't it? But many organizations waste resources, time, and energy trying to reach too many markets too far apart.

Try to be all things to all people, and you may just wind up being nothing much to hardly anyone.

CRAFTING YOUR MESSAGE

Once you know who your market is, you can begin to tell the story that will reach that market. Even if you are a retailer, even if you are a distributor or a wholesaler of widgets, your organization has a message. What narrative are you telling your target market about the products and services that you offer?

Consider the difference between Whole Foods and Trader Joe's. What differentiates those two stores? It's not so much their products. At either store, you will find high-end natural foods, many of them organic. There are differences between the products on their shelves, but strictly in terms of merchandise, there is more to compare between Whole Foods and Trader Joe's than to contrast. The difference between the two stores is the narrative that each tells about what it means to shop there. Whole Foods takes itself seriously and seems to expect the shopper to take it seriously too. Shopping at Whole Foods, you feel, is one small step toward saving the world. Trader Joe's, on the other hand, says to the shopper, "Isn't this fun? Don't you just love free-range chicken tikka? Ooh, you've got to try these organic potato chips." If you want to know the difference between two stores, don't compare the products; the real difference is in the message.

To align message with market is simply to communicate a message that resonates with your market. Given our market in Orlando, our central message at Calvary became *Real Church. Real People. Real God.* "This is not la-la land," we were saying with that message. "You're looking for something real; you will find it here." That message resonated. Our congregation grew from twelve hundred to thirty-seven hundred in five years.

As long as we're talking about churches, consider the difference between the message at an inner-city church and a suburban church. At the inner-city church, where the congregants know themselves to be on the razor's edge and where they don't always feel safe, the pastor says, "God will take care of you." At the suburban church, where the congregants' chief spiritual danger is that they will be *too* secure and comfortable, the pastor says, "You need God more than you realize." It's not two different gospels that the preachers at those two churches are preaching, just two different emphases within the same gospel.

ESTABLISHING YOUR MEDIUM

The third point of alignment is medium—the architecture, the dress code, the ambient music, the whole experience of your organization. Picture the interior of a Starbucks coffee shop. The architecture and furnishings are urban, hip, even if the Starbucks is sitting by the interstate outside a small town in Kansas. The music, the arrangement of the tables and chairs, the trained familiarity of the baristas—everything conveys the idea that Starbucks is selling an experience more than it is selling coffee. The message of Starbucks—that idea that urbanity is a commodity that can be bought and sold—carefully crafted to resonate with Starbucks' target audience of young professionals, is communicated in every detail of the physical setting.

Or consider the ways in which Whole Foods and Trader Joe's tell their respective stories through the medium of the retail space. At Whole Foods, almost every employee is wearing either the white smock that signals culinary seriousness or the black T-shirt that is standard issue for all earnest urbanites. Whole Foods' work clothes say, unequivocally, "We take this seriously, and you should too." At

Trader Joe's, on the other hand, everybody is wearing a Hawaiian shirt.

Think about the difference in medium between Moe's Mexican Grill and Morton's Steakhouse. Moe's is loud and fun and brightly lit. You walk in the door, and everybody behind the counter yells, "Welcome to Moe's!" When you walk in the door at Morton's, nobody is yelling at you. It's subdued and dark and wood paneled. They give you twice as many glasses and forks as you need. One medium is not better than the other; they're just aligned with different markets. Morton's is all about businesspeople with expense accounts. They expect to be pampered. They're paying (or their companies are paying) for everything to be overdone. But Moe's is going for college kids and young families that expect to fill their own paper cups.

The importance of medium is even more important in a church setting. If the market is young, creative city dwellers and your message aligns with their interests and needs, but the music is the same music they heard in the country churches they left behind, that's not going to fly. In church settings, people frequently conflate their theological convictions with their preferences regarding medium of expression. The stakes, therefore, are especially high.

CHANGING YOUR ALIGNMENT

In a turnaround situation, you are almost surely going to find that you need to change your organization's market, message, or medium—and likely all three. If you are going after a new market, you will have to change your message and your medium accordingly.

Or perhaps your market stays the same, but you will need to change your message and medium in order to reach that market better. If you are going to change market, message, or medium, you have to take steps to keep the other two in alignment. Otherwise, you can find that you have gotten way out in front of yourself, perhaps losing your old market without gaining a new one.

Dr. Paul Walker, my mentor at Mount Paran, used to say, "Don't be intimidated by fads. Get your operation in alignment, and expand carefully at the edges." Expand carefully at the edges—that's a key idea. It would not be surprising if you needed to make significant changes to your organization. That's what it means to be in a turnaround. But think long and hard before you try to turn things around by changing the core of what your organization does.

Say you have a company that manufactures and distributes nuts and bolts and other hardware, and you look around and realize that the landscape is changing; you realize that you would be better off in the software business. You announce that you are no longer in the hardware business, but you are now in the software business. The problem is that those who bought hardware from you aren't interested in buying software from you. Your message has changed radically and abruptly, and it is now fatally out of alignment with your market. Furthermore there are hundreds of companies that have been designing software a whole lot longer than you have. Even your most loyal hardware customers aren't going to buy software from you. So you've lost your old market without gaining a new market.

On the other hand, you might say, "Acme Hardware manufactures and distributes hardware. But we also sense that there may be a market for software that manages inventory in a hardware store.

We understand *hardware software* better than anybody else." You're doing what you do, and you're expanding carefully at the edges. That's where sustainable growth happens in an organization. Even in a desperate turnaround situation, if you shift your market radically and suddenly, you may lose the market you have before you can get a new one.

"NOT YOUR FATHER'S OLDSMOBILE"—A CAUTIONARY TALE

The demise of Oldsmobile is a textbook example of a company getting ahead of itself and changing its message before it had a new market to align with the new message. Management at Oldsmobile realized that it had a specific market that wanted a specific kind of car. For decades they had been convinced that there would always be people who wanted Oldsmobiles, and that those people would always want Oldsmobiles to look like Oldsmobiles. They did quite well with that market. The problem was that they were securing a growing share of a shrinking market. The people who wanted Oldsmobiles were elderly, and they were dying. Young people didn't want Oldsmobiles.

Seeing the handwriting on the wall, Oldsmobile hired an advertising agency to create a last-gasp, hail-Mary campaign to try to reach the younger car buyers who could give new life to the brand. The ad agency came up with quite a memorable slogan: *This is not your father's Oldsmobile.* It turned out to be the nail in the coffin for the Oldsmobile brand. Oldsmobile's existing market said, "Not my father's Oldsmobile? But my father's Oldsmobile was what I wanted;

it's what I've always had. I'm seventy-seven years old. If it doesn't look like an Oldsmobile, I don't want it." More to the point, that existing market had been looking for an excuse to break with tradition and buy a Cadillac anyway. It was Cadillac that benefited most from the *not your father's Oldsmobile* campaign.

Meanwhile, the young car buyers who were the target of the campaign looked at the new Oldsmobiles and said, "It sure looks to me like my father's Oldsmobile." The misleading advertising lost Oldsmobile its existing market without winning it a new market. That was 1988. Oldsmobile hung on another twelve years, finally shutting down in the year 2000. But *not your father's Oldsmobile* was the beginning of the end. All because Oldsmobile had let its message get ahead of its market.

EXPANDING CAREFULLY AT THE EDGES: A SUCCESS STORY

In my consulting, I often work with churches that want to change their market. Their congregations are aging, things seem to be stagnant, and they want a younger and hipper demographic. I warn them: do what you do well, and expand gradually and carefully at the edges. Make a radical turn to starboard, and a lot of your congregation is going to say, "I'm out of here." You have to give them something to hold on to, even as you work on finding a new market.

I know of a church in California that has done a remarkable job of keeping its old market—the graying stalwarts—while serving a new, younger market. I'm always dealing with churches that claim to have different worship styles in different services to serve different demographics, but this California church is actually doing it right. They are carefully bringing medium and message into alignment with a new and growing market.

The eight o'clock service specifically targets the elderly members of the congregation. That service has a choir with robes. They sing hymns and old gospel songs—the same familiar ones those members have been singing their whole lives. For years the pastor's father preached that service at least once a month. He was holding that market.

The nine thirty service is more contemporary and family friendly. The pastor takes off the tie he wore at eight o'clock and preaches in a jacket and open collar. Rather than a choir, there's a worship band playing more contemporary music.

By eleven-thirty, the youth and young adults have finally woken up. The third service is targeted at them. The pastor does a complete wardrobe change for this service, donning jeans and an untucked shirt. The worship team plays just below the volume at which eardrums start bleeding.

The eight o'clock service is what pays for the church. Those loyal old members, so faithful in their giving, appreciate the fact that they have not been forgotten. In a world of *seeker-sensitive* churches, they have a place that is sensitive to their needs too. The nine-thirty service is where leadership is cultivated and where the growth mostly happens. The eleven-thirty service is the church's future. In terms of offering revenues, that service doesn't pay for itself—not by a long shot.

I urged the pastor to merge all three services at least once a quarter. Why? The old people need to know that there's someone else out there. The nine-thirty families with their small children need to be reminded that there is a future for them at the church when their children are teenagers.

That's flexibility. It's not compromise. That pastor is lining things up with three different markets. And he needs all three markets—or, rather, all three markets need each other. As you examine the alignment of your organization, ask yourself a few questions:

1. Do you need to be reaching a different market, or do you need to do a better job of reaching the market that your organization has always sought?

2. What message is your organization communicating? What story are you telling? Does that story resonate with your target market?

3. Does your medium—the experience that a member of your target market has when interacting with your organization—tell your story, or does it counteract the story you are trying to tell?

CHAPTER EIGHT

STEP 4: CREATING AN EXECUTABLE STRATEGY

When Allied tanks were rumbling through Europe in the spring of 1945, the next management question for the Allies was, "Which bridge will let us get our men and armor across the Rhine and into the heart of Germany?" For the Germans, the next management question was, "How quickly can we blow up every bridge across the Rhine?"

Somebody neglected to blow up the bridge at Remagen. And more than that, the bridge was lightly protected. Only a single detachment of German soldiers was guarding the place. It doesn't take a military genius to figure out where the Americans concentrated their resources. Soldiers from the Ninth Armored Division and the Twenty-Seventh Armored Infantry Battalion captured the bridge, and men and armor started streaming across on their way to Berlin.

When launching a turnaround, the first strategy question you ask yourself—the strategy question on which all other strategy questions hang—is this: where are the bridges I can get my tanks across? You're looking for bridges that are strong enough to support the weight of the troops as they get closer to their destination. And you're looking for bridges that aren't defended.

Let me offer a couple of examples from my Calvary experience to illustrate exactly what I'm talking about. In one example, you can learn from my mistakes. In the other, you can learn from my success.

STRATEGY 1: THE WRONG BRIDGE

As part of my *institutional reality* campaign, I examined every system, small and large, in the Calvary organization, from Sunday worship to the back office to Christian education to grounds and maintenance to the singles ministry. It wasn't pretty. The great majority of those systems were badly broken. There was so much hurt and relational brokenness in that church, so little trust in the leadership, that it was hard to imagine which of the tools in my toolbox might work. A sermon series on rebuilding and renewal? They had learned much earlier not to trust their preacher. A church picnic? People in pain don't want a picnic. A building campaign? Hardly.

But there was one system that seemed vibrant and healthy: small groups. As moribund as the church itself was, its sixty small groups were thriving. Apparently that was where the church was really happening. It seemed obvious to me that small groups were my best bet for getting across the bridge and into the territory I was trying to capture. So, like General Patton concentrating his forces at the Remagen Bridge, I gave small groups everything I had. I put together a brilliant strategy, complete with printed training materials that I wrote myself.

Here's how it was going to work: because Calvary had such a storied past, we still had more visitors than you might expect every week. We also had a good many senior citizens (this was Florida, after all). So I put together a plan whereby every week the senior citizens—who enjoy talking on the phone more than most young people do—would call all those who had visited the previous Sunday and ask them if they were interested in joining a small group. Any visitor who admitted that he or she was indeed interested in joining a small group would be handed off to a small-group leader, who would call and extend a personal invitation to the meeting, which would happen on Thursday night.

I congratulated myself heartily for creating such a perfect plan. But a month into the small-group campaign, we weren't seeing any visitors joining small groups. Not one. We asked the senior citizens if they were making their calls. Yes, of course they were making their calls. The calls were a highlight of their week. We asked the small-group leaders if they were making their calls. No, they admitted sheepishly, they hadn't been making their calls.

Obviously there was something the small-group leaders didn't understand about the plan. So we ran them through the training again. When they were retrained, we gave it another month. Again, absolutely no growth in the small groups. I asked the senior citizens, "Are you sure you're making those calls and passing them along to the small-group leaders? Because the small-group leaders just went through training a second time, so they're obviously well prepared to put the plan into effect." The senior citizens insisted they were making the calls. So I asked the small-group leaders again: "Have you or have you not made the calls?" They had not.

I finally realized what I should have seen much earlier: why small groups weren't the bridge that was going to get me and my heavy machinery across the river. Small groups were strong all right, but they were strong because the members viewed them as lifeboats launched from the sinking ship that was Calvary Church. On Sundays they were just trying to survive. On Thursdays, when they met with their small groups, they were checking in with one another: *you still here? You still okay?*

Who invites new people to climb in the lifeboat when the ship is sinking? Small groups may have been the strongest system in the church, but they were strong despite the church; their strength did not point toward a strength of the church, but really the opposite. Small groups wouldn't be the bridge that I needed to get the troops across to the next battle. To put it another way, the bridge may have been one of the few still standing, but it was still guarded, heavily guarded.

STRATEGY 2: THE UNGUARDED BRIDGE

Not long after that debacle with the small groups, I was wandering Calvary's halls one Sunday morning, and I heard laughter coming from the other side of a closed door. It is depressing to remember how rare the sound of laughter was at Calvary during that time; it was rare and noteworthy enough that I felt compelled to open the door and stick my head in to see what was up. Ten or twelve men and women looked up in surprise to see me peering in at them. "Hello," I said. "What's happening in here?"

"Sunday school," one of the women said.

"Sunday school?" I repeated. "I thought we didn't have Sunday school at Calvary." We didn't. Not officially, anyway. When I was going system by system to figure out exactly where we were strong and where we were weak, I had specifically asked about Sunday school. No, I was told, there was no Sunday school. But here it was. I had seen it with my own eyes. A group of men and women had taken it upon themselves to conduct their own Sunday school. And, unlike the vast majority of what was happening at Calvary at the time, it was obviously working. It was one of the few places where anything resembling joy was happening on Sunday morning at Calvary. Here people were doing what you're supposed to do at church. They were discussing Scripture and engaging with one another, encouraging and spurring one another on to love and good deeds.

And best of all, nobody else cared about it. Nobody outside the class seemed even to know it existed. There was nobody guarding that bridge.

I reversed field, and I poured all my resources into Sunday school. I promoted my singles pastor to the position of pastor of education and gave him a year to put together the best Sunday school program he could. We didn't even have Sunday school for that year. It was all about preparing to launch a full-bore, well-organized Sunday school a year later, with well-trained teachers who would provide the best possible experience for everybody involved.

When we finally opened up the Sunday school, it was a roaring success. In a matter of months we were teaching fifteen hundred students—adults and children both—every Sunday. From zero to fifteen hundred in a church that, only a few years earlier, had only twelve hundred members. I had found the bridge I was looking for. All those visitors, who were still coming, now had an obvious place to plug in and get involved. It made a huge difference. I have already mentioned the television programs that attracted visitors to Calvary. But it was our Sunday school program that kept them there. It was our Sunday school program that secured the growth that the church so desperately needed.

That's what I call *executable strategy*. You have to figure out which system within your organization is that linchpin system that, once you pour your resources and attention into it, provides you with a *force multiplier* that allows you to make a disproportionate impact on your organization as a whole. At Calvary, my strategy revolved around Sunday school. At Southeastern, it was the admissions department. At ORU, it was chapel. In each case, an hour's investment in that system led to much more than the results one would expect from an hour of work. In each case, the system in question touched every other system in the organization, even if it wasn't the first or most obvious choice. Besides, the first, most obvious choice is frequently a guarded bridge. Avoid real estate being guarded by people who have been at that organization longer than you, the turnaround artist, have been there.

Also, when looking for the executable strategy that is going to leverage your whole transformative project, give yourself the grace to get it wrong the first time or even the second or third. An unguarded bridge, almost by definition, is a forgotten and remote bridge. Even as you dig deep into the institutional reality of your situation, it is possible that you will guess wrong, just as I guessed wrong about small groups at Calvary.

YOU: CHIEF DECISION MAKER

When we talk about executable strategy, we're really talking about decision making: seeing the facts, coming to conclusions, and pulling the trigger. Somehow, in all my coursework and reading about leadership, I missed an essential fact that became clear to me only in the school of hard knocks: an executive is a full-time decision maker. The more complex the organization you lead, the more your role is defined by making decisions. It's what I do. All day. *Where do you want me to put this? What do you want me to do now? We don't have the money to do both; which one gets cut? What is really important in this situation?*

It can be exhausting. And thankless. I think often of one of General Colin Powell's favorite quotes: "Being responsible sometimes means pissing people off."[1] When I was a young pastor, I had considered making a change that might anger some of the people at my little country church. I went to an older pastor, a great mentor in my life, to ask his advice. "Claude," I said, "if I do this, do you think I'll make people mad?"

"Oh yes, absolutely," he said. "It will make lots of people mad."

"Then maybe I shouldn't do it."

"Oh, good heavens," Claude said. "You've got to do it. It's the only thing to do. You didn't ask me whether you should do it or not.

You only asked me if it would make people mad. Yes, it's going to make people mad. But that doesn't change the fact that you have to do it."

It was great advice.

If you are decisive, you are going to piss people off. If you decide to stay alive tomorrow, that in itself is liable to make somebody unhappy. Once you settle that in your mind, it's strangely liberating.

To say that you are ultimately responsible for the decisions in your organization is not to say that you are entirely on your own. The more you can engage your team in a proper process for decision making, the better you will get at it.

The six-step process I use is simple, but it is sufficient for the most complex decisions:

1. Reduce the issue to its essential level.
2. Frame the question.
3. Ask the people who really know. Gather information. If you know experts, find them.
4. Analyze the risk/return ratio.
5. Synthesize the consensus.
6. Make the decision.

As Paul Walker used to say, "You don't have to know everything; you just have to know who to ask." If you want to gather information, you have to create an environment in which no one is afraid to deliver bad news. You can't shoot the messenger and expect to get good information the next time. And once you have the information, you have to boil it down to its essential level, evaporating everything that is not relevant to your decision. Then you figure out the real question.

Right before D-day, General Eisenhower had a fire hose of information coming in—information about weather, personnel, tides, waves, intelligence about the Nazis. He listened raptly, carefully considering what he heard. And then he boiled it down to the right question: "Gentlemen, the question is, do we go, or don't we?" It is easy to get swamped by information. A good leader boils it all down and says, "What is it that we need to decide right now?"

YOU: AIR-TRAFFIC CONTROLLER

Executable strategy is actually more complicated than just figuring out the right things to do. It also involves knowing what order to do everything in. The more complex your organization—the more planes you have taking off and landing from your runways—the harder it is to keep the planes from crashing into one another. It's your subordinates' job to fly their planes. But they don't always have the vision to see how their work fits into the big picture—when it's time to take off, when it's time to land. As the executive of an organization, you're the only person who has the altitude to see exactly how all those moving parts fit together. It's your job to say, "Now it's time for you to land. You there—you need to circle the city another time or two and give this other guy a chance to get his plane unloaded. You over there, you can start your engines."

Air-traffic control, you might say, comes down to making sure each of your subordinates has the airspace to do his or her job.

Consider the Little League coach who has one good outfielder who keeps running in front of the other outfielders and catching their pop flies. He's destroying teamwork and respect, and it is the coach's responsibility to correct and rebuke the young athlete.

Often air-traffic control comes down to deciding whether now is the time or here is the place for a good idea to take off. When I was at Mount Paran, somebody started a ministry to Atlanta's homeless. It was a worthy cause, but bringing the homeless, most of whom were downtown, out to the Mount Paran campus in North Atlanta didn't turn out to be a good idea. We used to refer to Mount Paran as St. Mink's and All Sables. But we soon had addicts urinating in the stairwells and frightening our members. As the homeless ministry grew, the conflicts also grew.

Ultimately, Dr. Walker identified a downtown ministry that was doing a great job of reaching the homeless, and he said "*That* is Mount Paran's homeless ministry." The financial and volunteer support from Mount Paran made a huge difference for that smaller ministry, which is still doing good work with Atlanta's homeless population. It was a win-win; the homeless were served much better than they were being served at the campus of Mount Paran. Sometimes leadership can be held in bondage to some idea that looks good but is the wrong thing at the wrong place at the wrong time. Bold leadership, willing to face criticism from legalists, is rare.

Dr. Walker recognized that homeless ministry was indeed a good idea, but he also recognized that the initial approach wasn't working. He faced harsh criticism. To the passionate people in the congregation who were driving that idea, he had to say, "I like the way you're thinking … but we need to land that plane over on this runway, not the runway you had in mind." And he did.

TOOTHPICK HOUSES: THE PROBLEM OF SCALE

I want to finish this chapter with a few words about what happens when your strategy begins to show positive results and your organization grows. Everything changes when you scale up. I used to think that a big organization was just a bigger version of a smaller organization. I now know that this is not true. As an institution or business or church grows, there is a point at which it is a different animal and not just a bigger version of what it had been. If I build a tiny house out of toothpicks, I might learn a little something about how a house is made. But I couldn't build a full-scale skyscraper out of toothpicks, even if I could find enough toothpicks. Toothpicks aren't strong enough; I would have to use steel.

Leading a large organization is not just leading a small organization bigger. The things that worked when the organization was small won't work anymore. If you treat it like a small organization, you will end up shrinking it to the size where that kind of leadership works. As your organization develops and matures, both in numbers and in sophistication of structure, you are going to have to develop and mature with it.

The question isn't really the size of an organization as much as it is speed and energy. Because there are so many more moving parts, things are happening a lot faster in a big organization. Consider

Newton's second law, which states that the energy of a body decreases as its velocity increases. It's a true law, until a body reaches a certain velocity, and then it's not true. Newton's second law, for instance, doesn't explain how particles move on a semiconductor. The law is right until it's wrong, and then the faster it goes, the more wrong it is. The laws of leadership that work at small, slow organizations don't necessarily work at big, fast organizations.

The most strenuous leadership discipline in the world is to grow a church from fifty to two hundred members, or to grow a company from half a million dollars in revenue to a million. That's when you have the fewest resources and usually the least experience. Newton's second law is working against you. Things move slowly, and as velocity increases, energy decreases.

But at some point the physics flip, and Newton's second law doesn't apply anymore. The easiest thing in the world is to grow a church from two thousand to five thousand members, or to grow a company from half a billion to a billion in yearly revenues. Making your megachurch grow—that's easy. If you have fifty thousand dollars to put into a Christmas morning worship service, it's easy to draw a crowd. Mass draws mass. In physics terms, that's gravity. The average American doesn't have the discernment to know whether a restaurant is any good. He knows only whether or not there's a crowd. "This food must be great," he says. "I had to wait in line an hour!"

The leaders of the big organizations get all the glory, but the laws of physics and the laws of leadership tell us that leading a small organization is the toughest job of all. If you can manage to grow, it eventually gets easier to grow. A crowd draws a crowd. As you speed up, it gets easier to speed up; which is to say, if you're struggling with a small organization, the best is yet to come. But as you speed up and grow, the things you used to do aren't going to work anymore. Even as you hope for growth in your organization, you have to expect growth and change in yourself.

CHAPTER NINE

STEP 5: SHIFTING CULTURE

America's self-image had been pummeled by the Vietnam War, Watergate, gas lines, Carter-era inflation, and the Iranian hostage crisis when Ronald Reagan came along with his winning smile and his wonderfully convincing optimism. Reagan did many great things for America, but one of the greatest was his casting of a new vision— a renewed vision—of what America was, what America could be. "America is too great for small dreams," he said, and everybody, including those who had voted against him, seemed to believe him. Reagan was our great Chief Culture Officer. He saw something in America that we had almost forgotten was there, and he said, "*This* is the truest thing about this nation." Reagan was America's greatest turnaround leader. He repaired a damaged dream, and the result was a new America. He said it best when he said, "It's morning again in America."

Early in my tenure at ORU, an outside consultant told me, "Dr. Rutland, it's not just that systems or finances are damaged here. The dream has been damaged." That was an incredibly important insight for me. In a turnaround situation, the biggest problem is never damaged systems or damaged finances. The biggest problem is a damaged dream.

The turnaround leader is the Chief Culture Officer in an organization. It is your job to create a vision and communicate that vision at every opportunity to every person who will stand still or walk slow! You are there to restore a dream or, perhaps, to create a new dream. At Southeastern, I created a dream out of thin air. At ORU, I had to bring an old dream back.

THE MOST JOYFUL PLACE IN THIS OR ANY PARALLEL UNIVERSE

When I arrived at ORU, it had been through a war. The question was how to bring joy to such a place. The obvious answer, I suppose, is to model joy. That's true enough. A joyful spirit on ORU's campus begins with me; no amount of talking about joy is going to do any good if I'm obviously miserable myself.

On the other hand, merely modeling the culture you wish to inculcate and not putting it into words is going to have only limited effect. If you want to anchor a new culture in your organization, it is vital that you articulate it as often as you possibly can to as many people as you possibly can.

I mentioned earlier that at ORU I do something unusual for a college president: I preach 85 percent of our twice-a-week chapel services. It's not because I think I'm the greatest preacher in the world. I don't even think I'm the greatest preacher in my own house. I lead the chapel at Oral Roberts University because it is a chance to communicate to the whole university what I want to tell them every week. And here's one thing I tell them every time I stand in front of them: "Welcome to the most joyful campus in this or any parallel universe."

Is it corny? Sure, it's corny. That fact isn't lost on me. Do students get tired of hearing it? Perhaps they do. But you can believe that they know what is important to me; they understand that from the top down, the intention and expectation is that their campus will be a place of joy. And by the way, every chapel at ORU is televised across the country, so anybody who's watching knows, just like the students, that ORU is the most joyful campus in this or any parallel universe. For some years people became confused about what was at the core of the ORU culture. You can be sure that they know now.

CULTURE VERSUS BRAND

Culture isn't the same thing as a brand. A brand is an organization's promise to the world outside the organization. Culture is internal. Culture is what the members of an organization believe their organization to be. Disney World portrays itself as *the happiest place on earth*. That's a brand. It's the image that faces the customer. The culture of Disney World is fully integrated into that brand, for it is the employee culture of Disney World that enables the park to make good on its brand promise. The clearest example is Disney's *ice cream policy*. If any employee of Disney World—no matter her position—sees a child drop an ice-cream cone, she has the authority to go get a replacement ice cream for the child. She may be sweeping the sidewalk, but if she sees a child crying over a dropped ice cream, she can—indeed, is expected to—go fetch a new one. Because, for the kid who has just lost the ice cream he had been looking forward to the whole time he broiled waiting in line for Space Mountain, Disney World isn't the happiest place on earth. When a Disney employee shows up with a new one, suddenly it's the happiest place on earth again. That's culture supporting brand.

Spirit Airlines, on the other hand, bought itself a world of bad PR over $197.00. Rigid rules and callous customer service have earned Spirit an ugly reputation with many fliers, but their unyielding response to one Jerry Meekins was a masterpiece of poor judgment and arrogant leadership.

Meekins bought a ticket, then upon his doctor's orders asked for a refund. First, Ben Baldanza, Spirit's CEO, stated flatly that no exception would be made, even for a combat veteran with terminal cancer. Then when Spirit's low customer service ratings came to light, he called such data *irrelevant*. Irrelevant? The lowest customer satisfaction ratings in the industry? Irrelevant?

Then a devastating email from Baldanza regarding a similar 2007 incident came to light: "Let him tell the world how bad we are. He's never flown before with us anyway and will be back when we save him a penny."[1]

No wonder that after the Meekins fiasco, an anti–Spirit Airlines Facebook page sprang up, and tens of thousands of people *liked* it in the first few days. Baldanza eventually refunded the $197.00, but it was too little, too late. The fear of unintended consequences, though real when granting exceptions to policies, can paralyze creative responses and destroy a company's public reputation. The risk of setting a precedent is a petty fear. The opportunity to make a genuine statement of your company's concern for its customers is huge and very real.

For our part, at ORU we make good on our claim to be the most joyful campus in this or any parallel universe by coming at it from a number of angles. At ORU we take a somewhat unorthodox approach, speaking of our students as customers. At many schools the typical attitude of a professor toward his or her students is, in effect, "I'm smarter than you, more experienced than you, and you're lucky to have the privilege of sitting in my class." The students at ORU have paid a boatload of money to be there. They are indeed customers, and they deserve to be treated like customers. The personal touch of ORU's professors, that willingness of veteran teachers with PhDs to understand that their students are human beings who deserve to be treated with respect, was crucial to the culture.

I was proud of the academic leadership at ORU that acclimated to this new view of customer service. An example was their willingness to place faculty members on campus on the Saturday of registration so that they could get their student advising done. This meant our young customers could complete registration without having to wait.

Customer service and culture creation can often collide with harsh budget realities. In an effort to curb expenses, some elements of customer service can take a short-term hit. To get over the hump somebody has to grasp the realities and be willing to step up to the plate.

When I did the reduction in force at ORU, we laid off some advisement specialists, and this could have set back our customer service goals. Yet for the next two years our freshman retention rate was more than 80 percent, a sure sign of high—extremely high—customer service. This was possible only because the academic community took up the slack and did it joyfully.

When the time came, the faculty did remind me that rehiring full-time advisers was a priority. Until that time, though, they did what I asked with an eye toward customer service. The growth surge in my fourth year at ORU was in part due to this cooperative spirit. We grew every year of my presidency at ORU by increasing customer service and creating a culture of joy. Keeping a larger percentage of larger classes (customers) got us there, and everybody getting on board with both my vision and my methods was the difference.

One of my fundamental convictions is that in a turnaround you have to have all guns in the fight. From the security guards to the deans, we pulled together to create a new culture.

My son and I were once visiting a church in Georgia, and, as we came into the town where the church was located, a big billboard loomed over the road, advertising the very church we were to visit. It depicted a multiethnic, multigenerational congregation singing and smiling and clapping, and, by the looks of things, those people were having the time of their lives. It had the well-composed look of stock photography. The slogan on the billboard read something like, "The happiest church in town." I nudged my son and pointed at the sign. "Let's see how well they match up to their billboard," I said.

I might have said, "Let's see how their culture bears out their branding." The billboard was branding, a promise to the outside world. The culture would be how things looked from the inside. If the church turned out to be a bunch of sour-faced people mumbling "A Mighty Fortress Is Our God," the billboard would not only have been false advertising—it would have been perfectly useless advertising. There would be no point in attracting people to an experience that bears no resemblance to the advertised church.

The church in question, by the way, turned out to be true to the billboard. But it's a common enough thing to see organizational branding that is utterly out of touch with organizational culture. Every time a clerk behind an airline ticket desk manages to check me in without making eye contact, I can't help but think sardonically of the old *Fly the Friendly Skies* slogan. They have a brand, but it isn't consistent with their culture.

KILLING THE CULTURE OF FEUDALISM

The point of all this culture making is to create what I call a *comprehensive* model of organization: everybody in the organization knows the vision, and every action, every decision is directed toward that end. Opposing the comprehensive model is what I call the *feudal* model. Feudalism is common enough in organizations of every kind, but that doesn't change the fact that it is toxic.

Perhaps feudalism finds its purest and deadliest expression in America's prison system. The United States has the largest prison population in the world—well over 2.4 million inmates. Have you ever wondered how so few guards manage to control so many prisoners? Mostly they don't. They simply preside over the warfare within the prison.

An American prison is in essence a feudal system in which lesser kingdoms—the Crips, the Bloods, the Aryan Brotherhood, Nuestra Familia—are constantly at war with one another under the watchful eye of a high king, represented in this case by the guards. The great fear of the American penal system is that the Crips and the Bloods will stop killing one another and unify. If the petty kings in a prison were to stop their turf wars and start working together to oppose the guards, America would be in deep soup. The authorities could not control them. There are a lot more prisoners than guards, and they're a whole lot more dangerous.

In a feudal system, the high king relies on a combative tension among the lower kings to prevent them from banding together and overthrowing him. Louis XIV of France, "the Sun King," built the fabulous palace at Versailles. It is certainly the world's greatest monument to royal opulence extant. It is also a monument to imperial *divide-and-conquer* manipulation.

Louis was the quintessential *imperial CEO*. When he came to the throne, the nobility of France was a strong political force, prosperous, influential, and largely independent. Louis set out to domesticate the nobles by doing two things. He required them to live at Versailles and at such a high level of consumption that they went bankrupt. This forced them to stay at that level only by his patronage. In other words, total subjection to the king or impoverished banishment from the addictive luxury at Versailles.

In addition, he pitted the nobles against each other in petty, shallow, superficial competitions for his favor. Louis created ludicrous ceremonies around his bedtime rituals (called *coucher*) and his morning routine (*lever*), and the nobles struggled, connived, and bribed their way into certain duties in these farcical nonceremonies. Who got to hold the candlestick while Louis climbed into bed at night? Who got to fetch and arrange his slippers in the morning?

Their total dependence on Louis and their constant warfare with each other over petty nonsense made them easily manageable, if utterly useless.

The imperial CEO who pits employees, divisions, and departments against each other is less about production or success than mere control. To be sure, Louis XIV built Versailles. But the cost ethically and morally was huge, and Louis actually planted the seeds of his company's (France) destruction.

Steve Jobs certainly had one of the great turnarounds in business, but for all his accomplishments and advancements, Steve Jobs could be a ruthless manipulator, pitting department against department in blatant internecine warfare. The environment around him was notoriously toxic.

To be sure, he created the iPad. But he is hardly a model of the caring servant-leader. Steve Jobs was a tech genius, but he could be a driver of men, a master manipulator, and a ruthless bully. Control at such a human cost is the tragic waste of an imperial leader.

In my decades of leadership and consultancy, I have seen dozens of executives who mistake feudalism for leadership. They believe that if they can keep the CFO and the sales department and research and development in constant conflict, they can keep control. Well, maybe—but control of what? No organization is really going to move forward if the leader's primary goal is keeping the inmates under control.

Of course, the feudal system takes more subtle and nuanced forms in businesses and churches and other organizations than in the French court or the prison system. But over and over again, I see leaders who encourage or at least allow the people in their organization to row their own boats in the hope that friendly competition or the *invisible hand* of self-interest will somehow lead to organizational greatness. What it leads to is a culture of manipulation and triangulation that the executive ultimately cannot control.

The head of customer service talks to the CFO about a computer that you, the CEO, have already said no to. The CFO gives her a wink and says, "I can take care of this for you." Then he comes to you and says, "It sounds like customer service really needs that computer; I've got some extra money in this category over here, and I think the added efficiencies will pay for the computer." It seems innocent enough. It's not the Crips and the Bloods. But the CFO has set himself up as the Cosmic Permission Giver. Why would that customer service director ever come to you again? You said no. But the CFO—that guy can make things happen. You got triangulated, and if you let it continue, your leadership will suffer. In a feudal system, the petty kings aren't just going after one another's turf. Ultimately, they're going after the high king's turf, too.

Feudalism takes three main forms in organizations: the parallel model, the perpendicular model, and the circular model.

THE PARALLEL MODEL

In a parallel structure, each *kingdom* in an organization does its function well, but there is no real connection among them. Each kingdom forgets that it is part of a larger whole.

Operation Eagle Claw, the failed attempt by the American military to rescue the fifty-two hostages held in Iran, was a humiliating instance of the parallel model at work. The complex mission involved Army Rangers, Marines, Air Force Special Ops, and Delta Force operatives. They were ostensibly working together, but in truth they were working in parallel—a fact that became painfully apparent when bad weather and mechanical failures threw the original plan into disarray and the decision whether to abort had to be made. In the absence of an overarching command structure, the Delta Force commander and the Marine helicopter commander came to a stalemate. The debacle grew worse when a Marine helicopter collided with an Air Force C130, killing eight servicemen and destroying both aircraft, because the Marines and Air Force weren't using the same codes and radio frequencies.

It was a low point in American military history; the worst of the difficulty could have been avoided, however, if the service branches had not been operating parallel to one another. Operation Eagle Claw did, by the way, give rise to the United States Special Operations Command (USSOCOM), which has coordinated multibranch special operations ever since.

THE PERPENDICULAR MODEL

An even more dysfunctional version of organizational feudalism is what I call the perpendicular model. In a perpendicular structure, those little kingdoms aren't just operating separately from one another. They are operating in conflict with one another. Their crossed purposes bring them into constant collision.

When I was at Southeastern University, I talked with a student who served as the youth minister at a tiny church of about seventy-five aging members. Within a few months, this ambitious, hardworking student had built a vibrant group of three hundred kids; almost none of them had any other connection to the church besides their young leader. It could have been a transformative moment for that little church. This youth leader actually wanted it to happen, actually tried every way he could dream up to make his ministry an engine of uplift for the little church. If the members of the church had embraced him, had they reached out to the families of those kids, they could have had wonderful new energy and growth. Instead, they resented the presence of teenagers and made it clear they weren't welcome. The teens left the place a mess every week. They left cigarette butts in the parking lot. Some of them had green hair. And they certainly weren't carrying their weight financially. It takes money to run a big youth group, and these kids weren't exactly major donors.

The senior pastor met with the younger pastor and told him he needed to slow down the outreach and focus on some *nicer* kids. The youth pastor came to me for advice on how to fix his situation. He told me his pastor definitely did not want such teens in church. "There's no fixing it," I told him. "Your goose is cooked. That pastor has told you what he wants. It's a self-limiting decision, but it's still his decision. The collision is coming." Three weeks later, the pastor fired him and shut down the program.

My student was in a perpendicular situation. His goals were at odds with the goals and purposes of the church he was trying to serve. There was no alignment: the youth program and the church had different markets, different messages, and different mediums. And the senior leader had no interest in creative expansion. The great train wrecks in organizations tend to come from that kind of perpendicularity.

THE CIRCULAR MODEL

The problem with a feudal organization is that somewhere along the line it loses sight of the meaning of its existence. People survive for the sake of survival and grab power for the sake of being powerful. In that sense, every feudal organization has a circular structure. But there are organizations in which the circularity is more pronounced. In certain churches it seems that Sunday morning services exist to fund children's ministry and youth ministry, which exist to attract families whose offerings pay the rent on the building so they can have Sunday morning services in order to fund children's ministry and youth ministry to attract families.

Television ministries are notorious for falling into circularity. You're on television to raise money to pay for television, where you raise money to be on television. After a while you forget which came first. Are you on television to raise money, or are you raising money so you can be on television? I don't imagine there are many television ministries that went on television for either reason. But somewhere along the line, too many organizations lose sight of the reasons for which they even exist. *Circularity* is just another word for the staleness that comes from a forgotten vision. There are no collisions or fights, but the organization is only going in circles.

The circular model is perhaps the most deceptive precisely because there are no collisions or fights to signal a problem. Things keep moving. People are astir. There is the *feel* of forward motion—without any. In the majority of organizations and to the majority of leaders, movement *is* progress. As long as everyone is busy, as long as people and things are coming and going, as long as we have the feeling of doing something, anything, then we are about our business. Frankly, it is better to be in a system that breaks down. In that case, you have the possibility of finding out that something is wrong, and you can fix it. In the circular organization, the dysfunctions hide behind the busyness. Activity is mistaken for progress, and announcing goals for achieving goals. None of it is real, of course, but it takes a wise and bold leader to see the futility and call it to a halt.

CULTURE WARS

I need to say one more thing about creating culture in an organization. There will be countercultural forces working against you. In every business, every institution, every church there will be people who don't want to change, or who don't want to change the way you want to change. An unfortunate truth—but one that you can't afford to ignore—is that your opponents will almost always be more energized than those who are on your side. Those who are on your side take the new culture for granted. But those who represent the countercultural force will rush to indoctrinate any new employees you hire—and there are always plenty of new hires in a turnaround or start-up. You need an intentional program that acculturates your new hires quickly. They need to know what your organization values, what's nonnegotiable, what is in flux. You need to exert more energy inviting new hires into your culture than your opponents will exert drawing them into theirs.

Within your organization, you are the Johnny Appleseed of the vision. Everywhere you go, you're scattering the seeds of a new culture. But it's not enough to sow the seeds and hope they grow. In His parable of the sower, Jesus spoke of a man who scattered seed all over the place. Some of the seed sprouted and flourished, but most of it didn't survive. The difference wasn't the quality of the seed; the seeds were all the same.

The difference was the soil where the seed landed. The seed that landed on the hard-packed road never sprouted; the birds carried it away like so much birdseed. The seed that landed on rocky soil sprouted but couldn't take root. The seed that landed in the weeds sprouted and rooted but was choked out by the weeds. The only seed that grew to fruition was the seed that landed on good soil—cultivated soil.

The quality of the vision and message you broadcast isn't the only factor determining the success of your vision. There are people who will never get it. You can't afford to sow on rocks and weeds. You have to cultivate soil that is receptive, where your vision can take root and grow. You do that by adjusting the mix of personnel in your organization. In later chapters I will talk at some length about the nuts and bolts of hiring and firing. Here I want to talk about maintaining the kind of environment in which the people who catch the vision stick around and the people who don't catch the vision go away.

Here's a hard truth about turnaround leadership: some of the people in your organization aren't going to be on board with your new vision. That's not necessarily a failure on your part. It's just the way people are. Your stirring speeches might change the minds of a few of the old-timers, but inertia is a powerful, powerful force. People tend to be committed to the way they've always done things, even if the way they've always done things is failing miserably.

I'm a firm believer in early retirement packages when you're trying to implement a new vision. Make it easy and attractive for the old guard to bow out gracefully. At the same time, however, there will be older staffers who do embrace the new culture; make sure they know that you want them to stay. They will be valuable and powerful allies.

Most organizations are more afraid of turnover than they ought to be. Especially in a turnaround, high turnover isn't necessarily a sign of ill health. It could very well be a key to success. As I shared before, in my ten years at Southeastern, 85 percent of the faculty went away. Only 15 percent of the professors who were there when I got there were still there when I left. That's an outrageous turnover rate, especially in the staid world of academia. But the turnover had to happen if the turnaround was going to happen. There is in every turnaround an element of culture war. If the keepers of the old culture won't be converted to the new culture, they will perpetuate the old ways. Your vision won't thrive in their presence.

The turnover at Southeastern did not happen primarily through firing. I didn't come in like Chainsaw Al, dismissing people left and right. Rather, as I consistently articulated a new vision and acted on that vision, those who were committed to the old vision eventually realized that they would be happier elsewhere. They just went away. No such faculty turnover was needed at ORU. At ORU I found an unrewarded but excellent faculty that truly wanted to embrace a new president.

Here's another important point about adjusting your personnel mix: when it comes time to make a promotion, look for the person who viscerally embraces your vision. That commitment must carry more weight than seniority in your promotion decisions. Be aware, however, that this policy can cause a lot of pain.

At Calvary Church, I promoted a relatively junior pastor to the position of minister of education—a position that had particular importance given the fact that Sunday school was the linchpin of my plan to turn that church around. The guy leapfrogged several pastors who had been there a lot longer than he had. Oh, and he also had a prison record. He wasn't the obvious choice for such a senior position in the organization. But he understood what I was trying to do at Calvary, and he was all in. Some of the other guys were deeply entrenched in the old ways of doing things—the old ways that sent the church into a nosedive. Truth to tell, my ex-con's outsider status was an advantage rather than a disadvantage in the new and improved culture. He didn't have the same commitments to the old culture.

Battlefield promotions are always costly. It's hard to salute the guy you used to sit around and cuss the officers with. From the day my new minister of education started, it was as if his colleagues were determined to sink him, to make him look bad. They wouldn't do anything he asked them to do. They talked behind his back and undermined him every chance they got. But he was doing everything I asked of him, and I stuck with him.

Within the year, everybody I bypassed in that promotion had left the staff. When those people were gone, that part of the church really took off. In other words, turnover in that case wasn't evidence of organizational sickness. It was vital to organizational health.

CHAPTER TEN

STEP 6: KEEPING AN EYE ON QUALITY

The late quality expert Philip Crosby offered a definition that changed everything for me. "Quality," he said, "is meeting expectations."

That hit me like a hydrogen bomb. If quality is simply a matter of meeting expectations, then there is no objective standard of quality for anything. That is not to say that there is no such thing as quality. It simply means that most of us think about quality in the wrong way.

Knowing that quality is a matter of meeting expectations is freeing in many ways. In another way, it binds us more closely than ever to the responsibility to communicate with others in our organizations—and with our customers and clients.

What makes a quality shoe store? Well-made shoes? Good customer service? Low prices? It all depends on the customer's expectations—expectations that are set in large part by the owner of the store. Picture this: Bob opens a shoe store in the poor part of town. He calls his store "Bob's Pretty Good Shoes at an Affordable Price for the Working Class Family." A single mom from the neighborhood drags her three boys through the door of Bob's Pretty Good Shoes and is greeted by a butler holding a silver tray. He offers her a flute of champagne to enjoy as she browses the hand-tooled Italian shoes (starting at three hundred dollars) that line the tastefully accoutred walls. Is Bob's Pretty Good Shoes a quality shoe store? No, because it sets up one set of expectations and delivers on another set of expectations. Bob may be proud of his Italian shoes and his fancy butler, but as long as he's telegraphing that his store is the place for affordable shoes, he can't call it a quality store. Another way to say it is that his brand (his promise) is a deception.

Much more damage in the world results from people leaving their expectations unspoken. In many cases, they don't state their expectations because they assume their expectations are self-evident and don't require stating. This happens all the time in marriages. Two people get married, carrying all these unspoken expectations. Each thinks there's an objective standard for what anyone should expect from a spouse. Neither states his or her expectations because, well, it's obvious, isn't it? Make me happy. Fulfill me. Give me lots of sex. Cook for me. Make me secure. Don't change. Change completely. When such expectations aren't met (and how could they be?) it leads to quiet seething, punctuated by the occasional outburst of anger.

If the key to quality is meeting expectations, you owe your employees a clear explanation of exactly what you expect. There is nothing unfair about telling your secretary that you expect all of your letters to be flawless. Griping behind her back about her making you look stupid with those typos and misspellings in your letters—that would be unfair. Your secretary may think she's a quality secretary because she answers the phone well. She has no idea that you couldn't care less about how she answers the phone. You've had it with her, and she thinks she's the best secretary ever. That falls on you, not your secretary. It's your job to state what you expect, not your employees' job to guess.

UNSPOKEN EXPECTATIONS: A CAUTIONARY TALE

I once flew in to speak at a church, and the youth pastor picked me up at the airport. On the drive toward town, I asked, "So, how are things going at the church?"

"Great!" he answered. "I've got the best youth group in Ohio. It is rolling!"

The next day, I had breakfast with the pastor before the worship service. I asked him how things were at the church. He sighed. "It's going well for the most part, but I've got to fire the youth pastor tomorrow. I'm not looking forward to that."

"The youth pastor?" I asked. "But just yesterday he said things were going great."

"That's the thing," said the pastor. "The guy's a failure, and he doesn't even know it."

At the time I assumed that one or both of the men was lying. I now realize that, more than likely, each man was appealing to an objective (and unspoken) standard of what a youth group ought to be.

It's not hard to imagine the scenario playing out something like this: when the youth pastor interviews for the job, the chairman of the deacons asks, "What are your ministry goals?"

The young youth pastor replies, "To win all the kids in this town for Christ."

It sounds like a noble enough goal. What board of deacons could argue with that? So they hire the young man. Things seem to be going well. The youth group is growing, bringing in plenty of kids who have never been in church before.

Six months into the youth pastor's tenure, the chairman of the deacons decides he'll go check out what's going on in the youth room. The place is packed. There's lots of energy in the room. Then the lights go down, and the band comes out to play some worship songs at a volume that kills all the insects within a quarter-mile radius. It's not the chairman's cup of tea, but kids will be kids, so he's fine with it.

Then it occurs to the chairman to look around and see how his fifteen-year-old daughter is enjoying the youth group. And there on the front row, right by the enormous speaker, his little girl is standing next to a boy with a safety pin through his cheek, his pants sagging five inches below the waistband of his underwear, and a skull tattooed on his arm.

About that time, the chairman remembers that he was never all that interested in winning all the kids in that town to Christ. The board of deacons had different expectations. The eight kids who were still coming to youth group at the time were feeling pretty burned by the three youth pastors who had come and gone in the previous two years. All the deacons really wanted was a low-key youth pastor who would stick around several years and love those eight kids back to health. But nobody had the courage to say that after the candidate had given such a righteous-sounding answer. They assumed that even if he said he wanted to win all the kids in town to Christ, he would get there and somehow intuit that what they really needed was for somebody to take care of those eight kids.

Or maybe it happened the other way around. Maybe the board clearly communicated that it was looking for somebody to care for the souls of eight wounded teenagers, and the candidate, desperate for a job, said he was on board, figuring that once the church saw how many people he brought in, it would realize that his way was the best.

My point is this: there's no such thing as a quality youth group. There is only a group that meets the stated expectations of its context. An outreach to juvenile delinquents isn't better or worse than an *inreach* to eight wounded children of the church. It all comes down to what the leaders of the organization expect.

COMMUNICATING YOUR EXPECTATIONS

It is important and only fair to communicate your expectations clearly to the people you lead. This requires that you know yourself what you expect. It is a good idea to formalize your expectations for each employee. What are your core values? These will probably be the same for all your employees. Which values are nonnegotiable, which are negotiable, and which are nice-to-haves? You may need to work with your board to work out these core values for your company.

Once you have established your core values, consider performance and productivity expectations. What length do you expect customer service calls to be? What do you want the office newsletter to look like? How many refrigerators do your salespeople need to move in a month? For a refrigerator salesperson, selling ten units a month might seem like great performance. But if the boss is expecting twelve units a month, ten a month is a failure.

Finally, consider ambience. How do you expect your employees to contribute to the work environment? Do you care how they dress? Do you care if they play music at their desks? How neat are you going to require them to keep their workspace?

The employee who doesn't like your expectations is always free to leave your employ. He is not free, however, to ignore your expectations once you have communicated them. By the same token, you are not free to seethe when your employees don't meet expectations that you haven't communicated. People can't meet your expectations if they don't know what they are.

THE GREATEST FAILURE THAT EVER WASN'T

If you were to list the five greatest product failures of the twentieth century, surely the Ford Edsel would be on the list. The Edsel was supposed to redefine the way people thought about cars. But when it was presented to the American public (with much fanfare) it was greeted with a yawn. They had been led to expect a groundbreaking technological and design marvel, but the Edsel wasn't all that different from the Fords that had gone before—or, in any case, not different enough for the public to be overwhelmed by it.

That much of the story is well-known. But I once had a conversation with a retired executive from the Ford Motor Company, and he told me some things that I didn't know. For one thing, he said that the Edsel wasn't actually a sales failure. It was actually a modest success. The problem was that Ford's executive leadership rammed the Edsel down the throat of everybody in the organization, and when it wasn't a huge success—when it didn't meet the expectations that the leaders had set for it—all the people involved backed away with their hands in their pockets. Senior leadership took the blame for what was assumed to be a sales failure, but it really wasn't a sales failure. The Edsel story was a story of missed expectations, coming and going. Was the Edsel a failure? Well, yes, but not in any *objective* sense. It was a failure only insofar as it failed to meet expectations. But then again, that may be the only kind of failure there is.

CHAPTER ELEVEN

STEP 7: MEASURING AND CELEBRATING SUCCESS

Nothing is more important to a turnaround than rolling up small, quick victories that build positive momentum and give everybody the feeling that things are indeed looking up. That change in attitude lays the foundation for bigger victories later on.

Financial advisers, when helping their clients get out of debt, often encourage them to start by aggressively attacking the smallest debt, paying only the minimum on the larger debts, even if the smallest debt has a lower interest rate than some of the larger debts. Now, from a strictly mathematical, financial perspective, you should always start with the debt that has the highest interest rate. In terms of pure finance, paying off a high-interest credit card balance is more important than paying off a twelve-month same-as-cash television purchase. But we don't live as strictly mathematical or financial beings. We are also driven by emotional and psychological forces, and there is something very motivating about making that last payment on the television and applying that payment to the next-biggest debt, and snowballing up from there. A similar psychological momentum is important in organizational change as well.

But while the emotional boost of quick, early success is important, from the perspective of the turnaround leader, that boost is not the most important thing about early successes. Those quick hits give you the opportunity to show your team members that they can indeed trust your leadership. It is vitally important that you not only put your people in a position to succeed, but also connect the dots for them, showing them that they succeeded *because* they did what you told them to do. That may sound self-serving. Whether it is or it isn't, I can tell you that connecting the dots for your employees serves them. It gives them confidence; they know that they didn't just get lucky. They succeeded because they are part of a team led by an able leader. They succeeded because your plan is working.

When I coached football, I found that one of the hardest things to get a new lineman to do is to keep his head up when he blocks. It's natural to look down as you engage your opponent. But a blocker who keeps his head up enjoys a huge advantage. It was one of the great pleasures of my coaching career to see one of my linemen get his first big pancake block after he learned to keep his head up. And every time it happened, I took great pleasure in saying, "See what just happened? You kept your head up like I taught you, and you see the results!" The real point wasn't "See, I told you so," but, "See, you can trust me when I tell you how stuff works." That reminder made my player a better, more teachable listener.

So don't be shy about taking a certain amount of credit for your employees' successes. When members of your organization succeed, congratulate and praise them. Then connect the dots for them; remind them that they succeeded because they listened to what you were telling them. This empowers those who follow you by giving them more confidence in your leadership. They listened this time, and success was theirs. Now they are more likely to listen next time.

MEASURING SUCCESS

It is vitally important to the success of your turnaround that you decide what criteria you want to measure and that you put mechanisms in place to measure those criteria. At ORU, I set a goal of five consecutive years of 80 percent freshman retention. That's a full 10 percent higher than the nationwide average. The freshman retention rate is the purest, truest indication of customer satisfaction on a college campus. The 80 percent was an ambitious goal, and there were some scoffers when I announced it. But I would rather aim for the moon and hit the fence than aim for the fence and hit the mud. And as it turns out, we have met that goal each year since I announced it.

Whatever you measure, you get better at, even if you miss your goal. By measuring it, you value it, and that makes a difference in your organization's attitude. It's like the Heisenberg effect in physics, which states that the very act of observing a system changes the dynamics of the system.

You don't have to limit yourself to hard data as you measure for success. Student morale is a top priority for me at ORU. That's a subjective thing, but I measure it anyway. After every dorm meeting I collect reports from my resident assistants and dorm directors. These reports give me feedback on every aspect of student life, especially chapel. And I read those reports—every word, every time. The result has been an uptick in morale. A big reason is that those reports show me exactly what to work on in order to improve my students' experience. Another reason is the simple fact that the surveys communicate to the students that the president cares about their experience. That in itself is a morale booster.

YOU: CORPORATE MOTIVATOR AND CHIEF REWARD GIVER

You determine the pace at which the people in your organization move. You cannot drive people faster than you can go yourself. I have been around a lot of big-time leaders. They emanate a sense of huge personal energy. For all I know, they go home and collapse at night, but when they are around other people, they express vitality. That vitality gives life to the people who follow them.

Of course, it is true enough that some people naturally have more energy than others. But you can cultivate a sense of energy that energizes the people who follow you. When I played basketball a hundred years ago, I found that in the fourth quarter, when I began feeling tired, I felt less tired the more I cranked up my output. It was counterintuitive, but if I ran more slowly, I felt more tired. When you are tired, run faster. It energizes you, and it energizes the people around you.

But motivation isn't a matter of driving people; it is more about setting an aggressive pace and rewarding people when they do well. The chief executive of an organization is the Senior Reward Giver. I'm not just talking about financial rewards. In some ways, nonmonetary rewards mean as much to the people in your organization as raises and bonuses. When your director of HR makes it through another insurance enrollment period, reward her long hours with a thank-you note and public recognition at a staff meeting. That may seem like no big deal to you, but it's a big deal to her.

Another mentor of mine used to write fifty thank-you notes a week. He called them *thank-you grams*, and he had special stationery made up for them. I admired his gratitude, but I was a little daunted by it. "I don't think I can think of fifty people I need to thank in a week," I told him.

"You don't have to thank them for something they've done," he said. "I often just thank people for being themselves." If he was watching a preacher on television who made a good point, Dr. Gray would dash off a note thanking him for enlightening him. If he got good service at the grocery store, there was another thank-you note. He exercised a lifestyle of gratitude, and it made a huge impact on the people around him. The thank-you note is becoming something of a lost art, but it is a great way to reward the people in your organization. It's no big deal to you. But I promise you, it will be a big deal to the recipient.

In the winter of 2011, Tulsa was hit by the biggest blizzard in its history. People called it *Snowpocalypse*. ORU was buried. Snowdrifts were higher than a man's head. Pipes burst across campus, flooding fifty rooms or more. The campus would have been paralyzed but for the herculean efforts of the maintenance and grounds crews. Some of them stayed on campus for a full week without leaving. They worked all day, collapsed onto cots at night, and got up and did it again the next day.

When the crisis was over, we brought all the maintenance and grounds workers onto the stage at Wednesday morning chapel. They stood there in their work boots, blinking in the lights, while three thousand college students leaped to their feet and cheered for them. If you're the executive of a business or nonprofit or the pastor of a church, you may be accustomed to being the center of attention. But for those guys, it was huge. When you drive a snowplow, nobody stands out there in the parking lot to clap for you and say, "Wow, you're really plowing great." Most of those guys don't have a college education; no doubt many of them feel invisible to the college kids they serve every day. It meant a lot to them to have so many students recognize their work and love on them. There was no need to bonus those guys. They had already earned huge amounts of overtime. That gesture of gratitude was an even greater reward.

In your position as leader, your actions are amplified; it's as if you are talking through a bullhorn every time you communicate with your employees. They hear your criticism more loudly than you mean it, and they hear your praise and thanks more loudly than it sounds to you. Use your bullhorn wisely.

PART III

BUILDING THE TURNAROUND TEAM

CHAPTER TWELVE

HIRING FOR A TURNAROUND

In his book *Leading Change*, John Kotter makes a great point: it is vital in a turnaround to make sure that new hires aren't screened "according to old norms and values."[1] You can't let the people who are devoted to the old ways do the hiring, or else you'll just start the old cycle over again. You're cultivating the soil in which your new vision and culture can grow. If you're the one in charge of hiring, you're going to need to go about it systematically.

You have to have a system that helps you hire the right person at the right time for the right job. The goal is alignment: not getting everybody in lockstep, but getting everybody moving in the same direction.

THE IMPORTANCE OF A SYSTEM

Let me first say this word of comfort: everybody who hires makes hiring mistakes. If you haven't already, you will someday join the bright host of those who have made a huge mistake in hiring. You will hire the wrong person at the wrong time for the wrong job. I have made plenty of bad mistakes. But I will say this for the system I am about to describe for you: when I have done my best hiring, this is what I have done. When I have done my worst hiring, I have ignored this system.

I call my system *Finder-Binder-Minder-Grinder*. The terminology is borrowed from big law firms, though I'm using the terms in a different way. Every organization needs finders, binders, minders, and grinders. They're all equally necessary, though they don't seem equally glamorous. You need to hire in such a way that you keep the right types in the right jobs. You don't often see a pure finder, a pure binder, a pure minder, or a pure grinder. Most people are a combination.

FINDERS

A finder is a high-octane, entrepreneurial type. Finders attract everything to themselves: energy, people, talent, money. They just seem to have that ability; it's almost supernatural. They're creative—they go out and generate work, so they're especially helpful in start-ups and turnarounds.

There are a couple of downsides to a finder. First, they're easily bored. If you have a finder in your organization, you have to make sure he always has something new to work on. You can't lower the ceiling on a finder. Second, when left to their own devices—that is, when they don't have somebody keeping them in check—finders have a habit of destroying everything they've created. They attract lightning. That's what makes them finders. Sometimes the lightning is exciting and energizing. Sometimes the lightning burns your house down.

BINDERS

A binder is the person who can bring order out of chaos. He binds up wounds, heals hurts. Think about a bookbinder: he takes loose pages that are scattered everywhere, gathers them into a book, and binds them all together. The binder is the organizer who makes it all work.

The binder isn't usually as celebrated as the finder, but the binder is the secret weapon. The politician is a finder. His campaign manager is a binder. The finder-binder team is especially important in a start-up.

MINDERS

A minder has a shopkeeper mentality. I don't mean that condescendingly. A minder takes great pleasure in waking up every day, sweeping off the sidewalk, opening the store, and standing behind the counter. A minder is a process person. It is the minder who insists that you have all the policies and procedures in place. It is the minder who makes sure the expense account reports are filled out correctly. All this feels like a slow death to a finder. Indeed, the conflict between the finder and the minder is one of the biggest conflicts you'll have to deal with in your organization. Each thinks the other is crazy. But you have to have both. This is especially important to remember if you are a finder yourself. You need those minders around you.

GRINDERS

The grinder is the guy who grinds out the work. He's not creative. He's not a star. But you have to have grinders. In a law firm, a grinder is a guy who cranks out wills. In a nonprofit setting, a grinder might be the head of the phone bank—always reliable during every pledge drive, always willing to pick up the slack if another caller (probably a finder pressed into service) fails to show up. Without grinders, everything grinds to a halt.

INTERACTIONS BETWEEN FINDERS, BINDERS, MINDERS, AND GRINDERS

None of these four motivational types works well without the others there to support them. As exciting as a full-bore finder is, he's a disaster waiting to happen if he doesn't have a minder keeping him in check and (ideally) a binder to serve as a buffer to keep him and the minder from killing each other.

If you have a finder in business development, he can charm the potential partners and convince them that partnering with you would be the best thing they've ever done. But he always runs the risk of alienating them before it's over. There are details to work out:

paperwork to sign and phone calls to return and contract details to hammer out. A pure finder struggles with such *details*. He just wants to do another power lunch. If you don't have binders and minders underneath, the finder is going to burn out. As I often say, if you have a high-octane finder at the helm and he won't listen to people, the very stuff he finds can fall on him and crush him.

You may think of visionary types as being finders, but that's not necessarily the case. Consider the eighteenth-century evangelists George Whitefield and John Wesley. Both were visionaries. But they were very different personality types. Whitefield, like Oral Roberts or Billy Graham, was a classic finder-evangelist. He was a human magnet with the kind of speaking voice that even David Garrick, the most famous Shakespearean actor of the day, envied. Garrick said this about the day he heard Whitefield preach on a street corner:

> He reached up those mighty arms, his voice seemed almost like a thunderstorm as he said one final word: "Oh!" Why, he could break an audience with that word! When George Whitefield said "Oh!" men bowed before the Holy Spirit like corn bows under the wind…. I would give my hand full of golden sovereigns if I could say "Oh!" like George Whitefield.[2]

That's a finder for you. His power to compel people is a resident gift. There's nothing compelling about the word *oh*. Unless, perhaps, it is spoken by a finder.

Consider, by contrast, John Wesley. He was five feet four inches. He had a high-pitched, nasally voice. The effectuality of his ministry had nothing to do with personal magnetism. If Whitefield was a classic finder, Wesley was a classic binder. He was an organizer. People think of Wesley as a great revivalist; in fact, he simply provided management for the revival. He looked around and said, "This revival is happening. How do we organize it?" So he established the societies and bands—the method—that came to be known as *Methodism*. Wesley was ruthless in preserving the organizational integrity of the societies and bands. You had tickets; you had to have your ticket punched. You didn't just show up at society or band. If you didn't have your ticket stamped, you were out. And Wesley himself would go to the meetings and check people's tickets.

None of it was very glamorous. And yet his evangelistic work had an even greater impact than that of his friend Whitefield. Whitefield himself recognized it. "My brother Wesley acted wisely," he wrote. "The souls that were awakened under his ministry he joined in societies and thus preserved the fruit of his labor. This I neglected, and my people are a rope of sand."[3]

Wesley's work may not have been as glamorous as that of Whitefield, but he was no less a visionary and perhaps more of a leader. So I hope you don't hear me saying that you have to be a finder to be a visionary leader.

Here's another lesson that grows out of John Wesley's story: the energy in an organization has to come from somewhere, and there's a good chance the energy isn't going to come from the binders and minders. If the leader of an organization is a binder, that's great for long-term stability. But where is the energy coming from? For all his organizational skill and willingness to work hard and steadily, Wesley wasn't exactly a dynamo.

It seems strange to say it, but Wesley was never really a Methodist. He was an Anglican, and if it had been up to him, he would have stayed an Anglican. He felt nervous about the whole revival thing even as it was happening. To Wesley's way of thinking, the proper place for an Englishman to preach was inside an Anglican church. He preached outside the Anglican church only because he had gotten kicked out of his parish church. And even then he didn't go very far. He went out in the churchyard, climbed up on his father's tombstone, and picked up his sermon where he left off, just a few feet from the church.

Wesley's secret revival weapon, as it turned out, was a weapon he didn't even want: field preachers. They weren't Anglican priests. They weren't especially well educated. When he heard about these men preaching out in the open air—nowhere near an Anglican church!— Wesley was horrified. He denounced them, not wanting anybody to associate his movement with them. But his mother came to him and told him that he was wrong about the field preachers. She dragged him to Spitalfields and made him listen to a field preacher in action. When he heard the eloquence and power and saw the crowds coming forward, he became a believer in the field preachers' work. Those field preachers provided the energy that drove Wesley's ministry. Wesley got over himself, recognizing that his personal preferences weren't the most important thing about the work.

A lot of binder-oriented leaders delegate the finding to other parts of the organization. That works, but the Chief Executive Binder has to bind it all together and hold it, or else things spin off. The binder senses that he needs finders, but he's got to have the muscle to hold it all together. How does he do that? By articulating some shared vision that holds people together.

KNOWING YOUR PERSONALITY TYPE

It is extremely important that you understand your own personality type. Are you a finder? A binder? A minder? (Very few effective leaders are grinders.) More likely, you're a combination of two personality types—a finder-binder or a binder-minder. The finder-minder would be extremely rare. Once you know your own personality, make sure you have people in your organization who will complement your personality and style. Are you a finder? Make sure you have minders who can put a brake on your enthusiasm. Are you a minder? Where is the energy going to come from?

Once you have the people you need to complement you, continue to hire for balance. Make sure you have grinders who can grind out the work. Make sure you have binders who can hold all those conflicting personalities, like the eggs in mayonnaise that hold together the oil and vinegar that would normally go their separate ways the first chance they got.

Adjust your interview process so that you can identify where your prospects stand on the finder-binder-minder-grinder continuum. If you're looking for a finder, ask, "Tell me about a time you started something from scratch. How long did it take you? How frustrated did you get in the process?" If you're looking for a binder, say, "Talk to me about a time you came into a situation where things were a mess and you brought order out of chaos. What was the hardest part? How long did it take you? How frustrated did you get?" If you need a minder, describe a situation in which there was conflict between the finders and the minders in an organization, and ask your interviewee how he would have responded.

Remember, alignment is not uniformity. It's not a matter of sticking people in the right hole. It's a matter of understanding who people are on your staff: how do they complement you? How do they complement each other? How do you keep their planes from crashing into one another?

Where we go wrong is asking people to do things they can't do. To return to our phone-bank captain, the grinder, if you ask that guy to find twenty-five new callers for the phone bank, he can't do it. You might as well ask him to start a new 501(c)(3) offshoot of the organization. That's okay. The same grinder mentality that makes him a great phone-bank captain makes it very hard for him to go out and find new callers. That's a finder's job. If a finder brings twenty-five new callers to your phone captain, the binder can get them situated in no time.

What I'm saying is that the frustration you feel in your staff may be your fault. You're asking the sun to be the moon. You can't be angry at the sun because it's hot; that's what it's paid to be. You can't get mad at the moon for being pale and romantic. That's just the nature of the moon.

A WORD ABOUT FINDERS AND MINDERS

As I touched on earlier, the number one area of conflict in your staff will probably be between finders and minders. The minder wants to see every *i* dotted and every *t* crossed. He wants to see the staff manual updated. The finder is intuitive and spontaneous. The minder says, "Have you thought this out? What is the contingency plan? Where's the budget?" The finder says, "Budget? I'm not talking about a budget! I'm talking about a project that's going to take this company to a whole new level! Why are you trying to rain on my parade?"

The finder, if he is smart, will tolerate the minder. It is the minders, after all, who make it possible for the finders to follow their passions. Being able to see a vision isn't the same thing as being able to make it a reality. Sure, the bridle and harness are a limitation for a horse, but they are also the means by which the horse's power is directed toward a useful end. Ironically, it is the bridle that makes it possible for the horse to cut loose; since it has someone to keep it from crashing into the rail, it can concentrate on running its hardest.

Though smart finders appreciate minders, it has been my experience that minders never quite learn to tolerate finders. A finder is a source of constant irritation to a minder. To the minder, the finder feels almost illegal, on the edge of ethics and law. "I don't know what it is," the minder says, "but somehow or other there is something wrong with this guy. It will show up sooner or later."

At ORU, I hired two executives from the business world rather than the education world. They were finder-binders with strong emphasis on the finder. To their way of thinking, things in a university setting moved at a glacial pace. They wanted *speed to market*. I had to keep them constantly on new projects for fear that they would tear all the stuffing out of the couch like bored dogs left alone all day. Another of my executives, on the other hand, was the quintessential binder-minder, demanding that every procedure and policy be in place.

All were very good at their jobs, but a major part of my job was keeping them from killing each other. I don't know how many times one would storm into my office, saying, "Do you realize this will sabotage my project? Over forms! Paperwork! I've got important things to do here. I can't be filling out forms!" Then, half an hour later, the other would be in my office, holding a very neat and organized folder.

"This form isn't filled out right."

"So I've heard," I would say. "But do you realize that getting all these forms filled out is going to slow this project down?"

Blank stare. *Tick. Tick. Tick.* "But it's not filled out right."

"I understand that. But filling it out right will add another day to the project. Is it absolutely necessary that we fill it out *before* we move forward?"

"But it's not filled out right."

As I mentioned in a previous chapter, a big part of the leader's job is air-traffic control. I was constantly trying to keep them from crashing into one another, always having to push back on them.

"This RFP [request for proposal] isn't right."

"I understand that. Can't we bend the rules just a little bit here?"

"Let's start building! Let's get a steam shovel in here."

"No, we should probably get a contract first."

It's no small thing to get a finder with a very low regard for rules to work with a minder who has a slavish, almost idolatrous regard for order. But the extent to which you can make those gears mesh, while tolerating the friction, determines your ability to create a powerful team.

CHAPTER THIRTEEN

THE TROUBLING ART OF FIRING

No one but a sociopath enjoys firing people. Nevertheless, if you are going to be a turnaround leader, you will find yourself in situations where you have no other choice. Turnaround leaders by definition find themselves in dysfunctional situations; people who have learned to survive in dysfunction aren't always able to function when normality is restored. In many cases, turnover is the turnaround's best friend.

Please understand: I consider firing employees to be a course of last resort. Even at Southeastern University, where we saw an 85 percent turnover among faculty, I didn't fire (or, more precisely, choose not to renew the contracts of) more than a handful of faculty members. Of those who left, the overwhelming majority left voluntarily and without rancor. Because I was consistent in communicating a new vision and consistent in holding all employees accountable to higher professional standards, instructors who didn't want to go that way drifted away, one by one. Others left for a wide variety of reasons, but we tried to *hire up* each time, taking advantage of attrition to bring on faculty members who embraced the new vision.

At Southeastern one administrator came to my office and said, "Dr. Rutland, I see what you are doing here. I see how you are raising standards. And I don't think I can play in that league. Would you give me to the end of this semester to find a job elsewhere? Then I'll clear out and let you get somebody in here who can do what you need done." I genuinely appreciated his honesty and self-awareness, and I gladly gave him until the end of the semester to find a new position—and even a couple of months after that.

As the story above shows, when you are honest about your expectations, and your team members are honest about their ability and their commitment, parting ways doesn't have to be a crisis or a drama. In the end, you have to articulate exactly what you expect from your employees. You have to hold people accountable. If you're going to turn a ship, there are going to be people who did things a certain way to get them into this mess. Some can make the change. Some can be retrained. But not everybody can make the turn. You need to communicate this to your staff long before it becomes an issue. Make sure they understand that at times you will need to make adjustments in the staff. Don't wait until there is a crisis before you educate them on how things will work: "From time to time there will be staff transitions—not now, but it will happen. I will evaluate constantly, and people who aren't performing and won't change will need to move on."

Conversely, you need to understand that when employees quit and move on, they haven't betrayed you. Your job as the leader is to work with the finders, binders, minders, and grinders in your organization to make their gears mesh together for as long as they can. But also know that people are passing through your organization. Your finders especially are likely to move on. Don't put your tent pegs in too deep. We're all leaving in the morning. Explore, celebrate, use people's gifts while they're with you. And when they aren't there anymore, new people will be. Don't get desperate, and don't be too afraid of the thought that some one person in your organization might quit. There are seven billion people on the planet. Somewhere there's another person with the skill set you need.

THE POWER OF ONGOING ASSESSMENT AND ACCOUNTABILITY

In an earlier chapter I discussed the importance of measurement in your organization. Only what you can measure will improve. We need to talk about measurement specifically in terms of hiring and firing. Especially in an organization that has been dysfunctional for a long time, the idea of measurement and accountability can be threatening. For people who aren't accustomed to being held accountable, accountability may feel like a pretext for the new leader to get rid of old staff. In a dysfunctional organization, in other words, employees may feel that they have nothing to gain from accountability.

Communicate to your organization that firing people is not the first goal of assessment—or even the second or third goal. A healthy organization is constantly in assessment mode, constantly diagnosing problems and fixing them. Firing people is one option—and your organization needs to understand that—but that option is relatively far down the line. Your real goal is to help your employees succeed, not to hasten their failure.

If your stated goal is to sell a hundred refrigerators a month and you're only selling fifty, why? Maybe you have two salespeople selling twenty-five refrigerators each. What kind of adjustments do you make? Maybe you hire two more salespeople to meet that hundred-refrigerator goal. Your employees need to understand that the assessment process that they fear might well lead to a bigger budget for their department.

But still, this process of assessment and adjustment may lead to a place where you have to say, "Look, Bob, we love you; this doesn't invalidate your place in the universe, but the expectation is that you were going to sell twenty-five refrigerators. We've retrained you; we've equipped you; we've added extra salesmen; we've changed the purchase order plan. We've tried to make it easier for you, but you still aren't meeting your sales goal. It's not the purpose of this company to keep you employed."

This is a very important point: it is not the purpose of your organization to keep unproductive people employed. You have a fiduciary responsibility to your investors or, in the case of a nonprofit, to your members and donors. You violate that responsibility when you hand over their money to people who are not doing their jobs.

Be aware that in a turnaround, you are probably coming into a situation in which nobody has been held accountable for quite a while. Not long after arriving at Southeastern, I asked one of the professors of homiletics—that is, the art and methods of preaching—to speak at chapel. The sermon he delivered was literally the worst sermon I had ever heard. Realizing that every preacher has an off day every now and then—and having had my share of off days myself—I called the professor to my office to discuss the sermon. I asked him, "So, how did you feel that your sermon went this morning?"

"I thought it went pretty well," he answered.

"Pretty well," I said. "Would you say that you did your best?"

"Yes, I would say I did my best."

"As in, if you had it to do over again, you wouldn't do anything differently?"

"That's right," he said. "I wouldn't really do anything differently."

"Let me ask you something else. If you could teach young ministers to preach just like that, would you feel content?"

"Yes," he said, "that is my goal."

"If that was your best work," I said, "I'm not going to renew your contract." He looked astonished. I continued, "If you are teaching your students to preach like that, you can't work here. I want them to be taught to preach by a professor who can model it for them."

You have to articulate what you expect.

While we're on the subject, I should mention that I think you should hold your new hires accountable within ninety days of joining your organization—especially in a high-level position. Ninety days is not too soon to expect a positive, measurable contribution to the turnaround.

I hired a high-level employee once and quickly realized that I had made a mistake. It wasn't working out, and I didn't think it was ever going to work out. The guy had moved to town for the job, and in a conversation he casually mentioned that he was planning to buy a house. I immediately told him to close the door. We needed to talk. An ancient proverb says you should plant your field first and then build your house, I told him. "You don't need to buy a house. Your field just isn't sprouting here." He was shocked. People usually are. But I didn't need more than ninety days to know that I had made a mistake. Don't keep carrying oats to a dead horse.

Such conversations are awkward. No healthy person wants to have them. So you put it off. But you can be sure delay doesn't make things any easier. They buy a house. It's that much harder to have the talk. Then their kids are in high school. Do you seriously think your employee is going to take the news better then? I hate to make hiring mistakes. The employee suffers. His family suffers. I suffer. But if an employee tells me in the hiring process that he can play second base and then, after being hired, he boots every grounder into the outfield, it's not necessarily my fault that he can't play second base. Again, I don't suggest that firing a person should be your first course of action. Adjust what you can long before you resort to firing a person. Maybe you can move your second baseman to the outfield. Maybe lots of things. Try those things first.

One dean at Southeastern just couldn't do his job. But I had heard that he had been one of the great classroom teachers in the history of the school. I called him into my office one day to talk things over. He sat there with the hangdog look of a kid who's been summoned to the principal's office. "You hate your job here, don't you?" I asked.

He slumped even lower in his seat. "You're firing me, aren't you?"

"No, I'm not firing you. I need you here. But I need you in the classroom. How would you feel about going back to the classroom?"

He was thrilled with the idea. He had taken that position only as a favor to the previous president—and supposedly on a temporary basis. Years later, he was still in a job he hated and felt unqualified for. When he moved back to the classroom, he went back to being one of the university's most important assets.

SOME THINGS TO REMEMBER ABOUT FIRING EMPLOYEES

Knowing that letting people go is an inevitable part of leadership—especially turnaround leadership—there are a few things you can do to prepare yourself ahead of time.

The first is this: realize that it is going to be painful. When you have a sore tooth, you reach a point where you simply have to pull it. But when you pull it, some healthy gum tissue is going to come out with it. This is especially true when you come into an organization from the outside. Everybody who was there when you got there has a head start on you when it comes to *karma* within the organization. Even after you've been there five years, you will not have *caught up* with those who were there first. When it comes to seniority, you never catch up. Firing that guy is always a risk. He has friends and connections in the organization that you may not even know about. But that doesn't mean you shouldn't fire him.

As Sollozzo said in *The Godfather*, "Blood is a big expense."[1] Are you willing to pay that price? That's not a rhetorical question. You have to decide if the price is worth it. So how do you make that calculation? Here are a few questions I always ask:

1. Is this a crisis that I have to deal with now?
2. What happens if I delay action? Will delaying make things worse? Might it make things better?
3. Do I have the emotional, spiritual, and financial resources to deal with this situation now?
4. Is there some other solution besides firing?

Also, there are a few housekeeping matters you need to tend to in order to minimize the pain and expense of firing once you realize that it is necessary. First, communicate with your employees regarding their performance. Confront them when they are not doing their jobs, and document those confrontations. Ask them to sign the document and keep it in a file. It should never come as a surprise to an employee when you fire him.

Second, stay in touch with your board so you can be sure it has your back, especially if you are firing someone who is high in the organization or who has been there a long time.

Third, know the labor laws in your state. If you are in an at-will state rather than a right-to-work state, that is a huge benefit. In at-will states, you don't have to tell an employee why you are firing him. I recommend that you don't. It might save you on lawsuits later.

Finally, once you have paid the price of firing an employee, hire well so as to avoid starting the cycle all over again. Try to take advantage of all openings to *hire up*.

I'm not nearly as squeamish as I used to be about firing people. I hate layoffs as a means of bottom-line cost control. That just feels penny ante to me, but sometimes it's necessary. But firing because an employee isn't performing—that may be a wise and necessary move. It's worth remembering that the world is full of people who would be happy to do a great job for you. There's no point letting a nonperformer hold that spot down. And furthermore, you should remember that getting fired for performance is often the best thing that ever happens to some people. It cuts them loose to find something that they are really suited for, and frequently it's the wake-up call they need to get themselves in order.

In a classic Peter Principle move, I promoted one of the best field workers in my international relief organization into an administrative position at the home office. He failed—and badly. When I fired him, it was a miserable experience. We were old friends; our wives were close. He felt hurt, just as you would expect. But from my organization he went on to finish his PhD, and now he is a very respected professor. He could have never found that calling as long as he was languishing in the home office of Global Servants, doing mediocre work in a job he hated.

If you fire people well, you will find that your staff adjusts itself without your having to fire all that many people. As you hold people accountable and hire stronger employees, you raise expectations, and those who can't meet those expectations go someplace where they can meet the expectations.

CHAPTER FOURTEEN

FORMING A BOARD

In *Leading Change*, John Kotter wrote, "Organizations that fail to anchor change in corporate culture most often do so because of a failure to assemble a sufficiently powerful guiding coalition."[1] That idea of a "guiding coalition" is incredibly important. The greater the change you want to anchor in the culture of your institution, the more people of substantial influence you need on board, and especially on the board. You have to get people around you who are in agreement with the change.

When an organization is in need of a turnaround, it is imperative that the board and the leadership of that organization be a powerful guiding coalition. In large part, this will be a result of how you lead and manage. This is an issue separate from your official relationship to the board. You must understand how your board thinks and analyze how you relate to it in light of that understanding.

THE INNER VOICE OF THE BOARD: EMOTIONAL, LEGALISTIC, HOLISTIC

Every board has an inner way of hearing that filters everything it perceives. Call it their inner *zeitgeist*. It speaks to them in every issue, every crisis, every circumstance. The things that voice says to them determines what they see—and therefore how they respond.

I divide this inner voice into three categories: the emotional, the legalistic, and the holistic.

THE EMOTIONAL

An emotional inner voice doesn't mean that the people on the board cry easily. It means that their inner voice urges them to respond out of emotion; and since emotions change, you don't know how they are going to respond in any given situation. An emotional board is an unpredictable board.

An emotional board doesn't respond out of law or ethics or precedent. They deal with each individual incident in isolation. They don't connect it with anything else. They respond to Crisis A one way. So when Crisis B comes along, looking for all the world to you like Crisis A, you think you know what they are going to do. But they go the other way because Crisis B makes them *feel* different from Crisis A. It isn't the crises themselves that determine how the board feels, but unrelated circumstances that may have nothing to do with the crises.

An emotional board isn't just unpredictable, but undependable. When the chips are down, an emotional board may back you, or it may not. You don't know, because they aren't operating out of an established core. You don't know what they are anchored to. To put it another way, you don't know their ethos. And if you don't know the ethos of a board, you can't depend on it.

THE LEGALISTIC

The second inner voice is that of the law, of legalism. *Law* and *legalism* mean specific things in the church world. But I'm not talking about the kind of legalism that concerns itself with makeup or hemlines or dancing or the movies. When I say *legalism*, I am talking about a philosophy that reduces the entire world to a set of if/then propositions. Legalism doesn't necessarily have anything at all to do with rabbinical law or religious doctrine. I've known plenty of agnostics who were raving legalists when it comes to health food or recycling or bottled water (first they were legalistic about making sure they always drank it; then they were legalistic about making sure they never drank it).

By if/then propositions, I simply mean the belief that *if* I do this, *then* that should always happen as a result. I said that this isn't necessarily a religious proposition, but I have to admit that religious settings are hothouses for this kind of thinking. Take child rearing, for example. Legalists love this verse from Proverbs: "[If you] train up a child up in the way he should go, [then] when he is old he will not depart from it" (Prov. 22:6). So if your child goes astray for a while, the legalist believes you should resign your position in the church. You shouldn't be a pastor if you have a wayward teenager, because his rebellion is proof that you didn't raise him right. That is legalism in a nutshell.

A legalistic board, then, is one that listens to an inner voice that says, *If you do this, then that will happen.* If that doesn't happen, somebody broke the law and needs to be punished. The voice of the law, left unchecked, creates a board culture marked by judgment and by a constant search for the reasons why something went wrong, even when the cows are out of the barn and they would be better off rounding up the cows rather than figuring out who left the door open.

The nice thing about a legalistic board is that it is predictable. Unfortunately, it can also be cruel, judgmental, merciless—all those things that go with the law.

THE HOLISTIC

The third inner voice is what I call the holistic or balanced board. Living in the tension between the voice of emotion and the voice of the law, the balanced board is able to function in crises that would bog down either the emotional board or the legalistic board. For instance, if the external audit comes back with a couple of management issues, the first thing the balanced board says is, "Okay, let's fix them. Let's get them right."

The legalistic board sees the two management issues on the audit letter, and it ignores the fact that the two things are easily corrected; it ignores the fact that the CFO pointed them out before the audit ever happened. No, it wants the CFO fired. "If he had done his job right, then we would have a clean management report. Therefore he broke the law." Well, no, he didn't break the law. He may have made a mistake, which is a very different thing. In fact, it may not have been his mistake at all.

The emotional board might say, "Oh, we don't care about a little thing like an audit. We're sure you meant well." *Or*, since the emotional board is unpredictable, you never know how it's going to respond. It might say, "Two management issues? Do you realize how bad you've made this company look? This is infuriating! You're fired!"

Your job as a leader—one of your many jobs—is to identify which inner voice your board is listening to, whether emotional or legalistic, and move it toward wholeness and balance. To the legalistic board you say, "Yes, of course there are laws. Of course we want to do the right thing. We don't want to cheat the public or steal money or defraud the government. If there are employees doing things wrongly, we want to get them right or move them. But look at the big picture. Look at what is really important—making things right, not punishing or blaming or giving ourselves the appearance of being especially tough on crime." That's exactly when the voice of legalism starts shouting, by the way—when you try to introduce a balanced and holistic voice.

To the emotional board you say, "I understand why you feel that way. I feel the same way myself. But soothing our feelings isn't the most important thing here. There are legal issues, ethical issues, questions of justice for everybody involved. Look at what is really important: making things right. That takes precedent over our feelings."

The issue is flexibility versus rigidity. The twenty-first-century flex leader will be infuriating to rigid legalists and unsatisfying to emotional boards unable to respond creatively out of a presiding value. Flex leaders can look whimsical to some.

The story of David Colbeth and his company, Spyglass, which is well documented in the *Ivey Business Journal*,[2] is a prime example of flexible reinvention. Spyglass began as a start-up by a small cadre of professors at the University of Illinois. They sold graphic modeling software to fellow scientists. After only a brief time and limited growth, the Spyglass team reinvented itself by entering the Internet world with some exotic new software. They exploded in growth and went public, but predictably they were soon snowed under by huge firms like Microsoft.

Colbeth's team reinvented Spyglass yet again as a high-octane, high-tech consultancy. Three major corporate reinventions in only five years is a challenging leadership hurdle, yet Colbeth managed it and then sold Spyglass for 2.5 billion dollars.

The secret, beyond some brilliant technical minds, lies in Colbeth's motto: "A bend in the road is not the end of the road unless you fail to make the turn."

Colbeth had to be comfortable enough in his own skin to turn and keep turning at such a high rate of speed. He also had to be brave enough to make those turns without being paralyzed by fear of turning Spyglass over.

Remember: negotiating the turns and maintaining the creative flexibility to reinvent your company or organization—while exciting and challenging to you—will be threatening to company legalists. They may drag their feet because of their fear. They may also rise up and oppose the reinvention as an out-and-out compromise.

"This is not how we started out!"

"This is not what you said last year!"

"The last time we turned I thought that was it. When will we go straight and quit this turning?"

The answers in order are:

1. No, it isn't. We are no longer where we started.
2. No, it isn't what I said last year. This is this year.
3. Brace yourself. We will turn every time we need to.

This takes courage. The accusations will come: there will always be the veiled accusation that the reinvention is compromise. You will hear that you're not being faithful to the original vision, purpose, and direction—something sacred to them. These charges and others like them will come.

When we began to reinvent Southeastern University as a transdenominational school, the idea caught on, and in ten years the enrollment more than tripled. But the growth was largely among students from outside the denomination with which SEU was affiliated. While this was exciting to most, that percentage of students being from outside the denomination was threatening to others.

I was convinced of two things. First, that we could negotiate the reinvention without compromise. Second, that those who saw this *outsider* trend as a dangerous compromise would never be able to weather the storm of the further reinventions that were necessary. The university had to make that initial turn and keep turning without losing sight of the nonnegotiables of its culture. I knew we could do it, and we did. Not everyone was happy, but this is the price of change—which is the leader's primary role.

The perfect example of a holistic approach is when the woman taken in adultery was thrown before Jesus (John 8:2–12). The Bible is very graphic about what happened. The woman was caught in the act. *In flagrante delicto*. She was dragged out of an adulterous bed and thrown at Jesus's feet. And, frankly, Jesus seemed to be somewhat unconcerned with the seriousness of her sin.

"You committed adultery? Well, don't do that anymore. Go thy way and sin no more. Where are those who condemn you?"

"Gone, every one, sir."

"Neither do I condemn you. Go home."

Can't you picture it? Everybody must have said, "Now we know who Jesus is. He's soft on sin. We've got Him pegged."

Then Jesus went to the temple, and there were the money changers. Their biggest crime was jacking up the price of turtledoves. And Jesus wigged out. He screamed at them, called them names, kicked over their tables, and ruined their merchandise, all the while whipping them with a piece of rope He had braided into a whip. And the money changers had to be wondering, *Whatever happened to "Go your way and sin no more"?*

A balanced, holistic approach is going to come up with different solutions to different situations. It's not as predictable as the legalistic board. But it is more dependable than the emotional board because the holistic approach sees the big picture.

The holistic church board is able to say, "Okay, Jimmy the pianist has gotten involved with a woman in the church. That's wrong. How do we handle this? What do we do with him?"

The legalistic board knows exactly what to do. It doesn't require a lot of thinking: "Fire him. Read a statement from the pulpit. Make sure everybody knows we don't put up with this sort of thing."

The holistic leader says to that board, "We have lawyers to deal with. If we make it public, he may sue. The woman may sue. Her husband may sue. We have to deal with a number of sensitive issues here. The woman has kids in the church. We have the youth choir to deal with. Maybe we can ease him out the side door and let him go quietly."

The legalist says, "No, no. We want a public execution. We want public disgrace. Cut off his hands. Send him out the back door."

"What about the lawyers?"

"Jesus was opposed to lawyers."

You're going to have to do battle with the legalistic board, because it can't respond with balance. It can't respond with grace. It isn't whole.

With an emotional board, you might look for a way to short-circuit the emotional part of the situation. You may go to the board and say, "Look, I don't want to go into all of this. Haven't I been your pastor for ten years? Don't you trust me? Trust me when I tell you that we are going to have to let Jimmy go. I'm going to give him a month's pay, and he's not going back to choir practice on Sunday night.

"I'm not going to say much else about it, but know that I'm not keeping secrets from you. There's a difference between being secretive and being confidential. I'm being confidential here. I need the board to understand that Jimmy has failed, and we're going to have to let him go, but I'm not going to make a big public thing out of it."

Your emotional board might say, "We love Jimmy. You're just jealous because he's more popular. You're intimidated. You're trying to run Jimmy out on a rail."

You answer, "No, I am not trying to run Jimmy out on a rail. There is a man in the next room carrying a handgun, and he wants to have a few minutes with Jimmy. I'm thinking that letting Jimmy go is better than murder in the lobby."

The legalistic board jumps to an answer far too quickly. The emotional board turns into a zoo. But the balanced board is able to take into account the whole situation. People used to talk about making kids well-rounded. The well-rounded board is able to take a 360-degree view. What about the congregation? What about the staff? What about Jimmy? What about the woman? Her poor husband? Her kids?

Move your board toward balance and wholeness. You start that process by understanding where they are now and pushing them toward the place they need to be.

GOOD BOARDS, BAD BOARDS, UGLY BOARDS

Let me conclude by summarizing the good, the bad, and the ugly of boards.

A GOOD BOARD

A good board provides three main things to you and your organization:

> Accountability
> Affirmation
> Resources

A good board holds you accountable to tell the truth about your institutional reality. Part of the board's job is to measure your location without being location focused. What are the real numbers—revenues, expenses, traffic, attendance, debt? What data are most significant? In many cases, your board is better situated than you are to know which questions to ask.

A good board affirms your vision and affirms your leadership. It is a difficult and emotionally sterile experience to work at peak performance year after year and not hear affirmation from your board. Just as you need accountability to keep you on the right path, you need to hear from the board when you are doing things right. This should be done formally and informally. Formally, with resolutions, letters of commendation, and even bonuses. Informally with letters, phone calls, and all the customary means of expression. I'm not talking about ego stroking. I'm talking about the same kind of honest assessment that they offer when they hold you accountable.

By the way, just as it is the board's job to affirm the leader and his vision, it is the leader's job to affirm those below him in the organization. Everybody wants a loyal staff. You earn that loyalty by being loyal to them. You have to take care of your people by affirming them and encouraging them.

Third, a good board provides resources. When you recruit people to serve on the board, you are recruiting them because they bring work, wisdom, or (in the case of a nonprofit board) wealth. You need people on your board who know things you don't know. The old guy on your board who keeps asking questions that you find hard to answer or that you would rather not answer may not be the Antichrist. He might just be trying to keep you from driving your truck off a cliff. You also need people on the board who are willing to get in there and work elbow-to-elbow with you.

And if you are the head of a nonprofit or a church, I need to be frank with you: you need people on your board who will supply wealth to your church or organization. There's no reason to be squeamish about this. You have to be careful not to be indebted to any one person in an unbalanced way, but you need people on your board who can and will fund your vision.

A BAD BOARD

If a good board provides accountability, affirmation, and resources, what does a bad board look like?

A bad board is obstructionist. Out of fear or tradition or woundedness, they want to stop momentum. Or maybe they are just unengaged.

Worse than the obstructionist board is the enabling board. This is often the nature of a founder board. If you are leading a turnaround and find a founder board still in place, you have your work cut out for you. I call them *yeah, yeah* boards. They meet. They eat supper. They don't ask hard questions. They say, "Yeah, yeah, let's eat and go home." An enabling board makes decisions that fuel incompetence or bad ethics or bad financial decisions or ego. There is a big difference between affirming a leader and enabling his vaunted ego.

THE UGLY BOARD

Finally, there is the ugly board. The ugly board has quit being trustees or directors or deacons and has become a management board. They want to manage the organization—especially if the organization is a church or a nonprofit. They want to run the choir and the youth group or the 5K fund-raiser or the donors' dinner. They are always in the way.

The ugly board is intrusive. They overreach, make decisions they shouldn't, and reverse directions made by management. They are trying to take over functions of the organization. They're in your life. They're in your office. They're in your hip pocket. They are demanding and unrewarding. They limit creativity, hinder innovation, and confuse your staff. The staff is unsure whose orders to take because the board meddles in operations.

The best board is engaged but understands its limitations. A good board knows that it is the board and that you are the leader. It empowers you to do what you do best.

THE INNER LIFE OF THE TURNAROUND LEADER

I like George W. Bush and admire many things about him, but I have to acknowledge that May 1, 2003, wasn't the best day of his presidency. That was the day he made a speech on the aircraft carrier the USS *Abraham Lincoln* in front of a banner that read *Mission Accomplished*. It was the end of major combat operations in Iraq that he announced. And it was true that the conventional phase of the war in Iraq was over by May 2003. However, the real fighting hadn't even started yet. American troops would be fighting and dying in Iraq for another eight years, dealing with a guerrilla insurgency that was far more dangerous than the army of Saddam Hussein.

Bush had fallen into one of the classic errors of the turnaround leader: he declared victory too soon. Why did he do it?

Everyone knows about the agony of defeat, but there is also an agony of victory. Success is exhausting for a leader. There is a temptation any time you enjoy success to camp out there. You want to stop for a little while and rest. You want to congratulate yourself, unfurl the *Mission Accomplished* banner, and hang it on an aircraft carrier. But just as no defeat is final, neither is any victory. You have to keep pushing. The minute you stop moving forward, you start going backward.

We are all tempted to declare victory too soon and engineer an end to the fight, largely because we become overwhelmed by the price that leadership demands. It all becomes too exhausting: the pain is too much, the sacrifice too dear. We should remember this: the expenditure of personal, spiritual, physical, and psychological energy by the senior leader is the number one factor in changing the course of an organization. This means that change is going to cost you—personally. True, some people are naturally more high-energy than others. When they walk into a room, you can almost hear the *swoosh* of their energy. Yet even for these people there is a *spending* of precious fuel as they lead. There is always a cost. If we don't consider it before we begin to lead, then the cost may catch us by surprise midcourse. Emotional and mental exhaustion can lead to a dangerous level of toxicity.

Too few of the leadership books, seminars, websites, and experts today talk about this matter of the price. Being a leader is hard. It demands huge sacrifices, is often lonely, and almost no one takes an emotional beating like a leader. Write this down: you're going to get hurt. You are going to get rejected. You are going to be insulted. This is what leadership can mean. And when it does, you can't bleed all over your staff. I would suggest that you should not even bleed all over your spouse. Your spouse, too, deserves sanity. You can, though, bleed on God. In the life of a leader there is a vacuum that only God can see, that only God can fill. No one in your life will ever fully understand; no one but God will ever see all. This is why I believe that leadership is an opportunity to know God at a deeper level. The great leaders learn to rely on God to sustain them when nothing of this world can. And this, too, is the price—and the privilege—of leadership.

Oh, and you can also get a dog. Harry Truman once said, "If you want a friend in Washington, get a dog." The same is true of most leadership roles. A dog may be your best friend by the time you're done.

Have I scared you yet? I hope so. We need sober leaders who have counted the cost. If you are truly a committed leader, your golf score won't be as good as it could be. You will likely give up time with your children. Most leaders' marriages suffer added stress. And leadership will also cost you friends. I must say, however, that most people don't have as many friends as they think they do anyway. If you make it through life and you have two or three close friends, you're actually ahead of the average.

Here's the thing: there's a cost to everything in life. If you go to the store to buy a candy bar, you have to pay the price for that small pleasure. If you get to the store and decide you don't want to pay the price for the candy bar, there is another cost. It cost you the candy bar. College is going to cost you a hundred thousand dollars or more. You don't want to pay that price? Fine. But now you must live a different kind of life, one without a degree. That's going to cost you too. Every decision has a price. This principle is what economists call *opportunity cost*.

The costs of effective leadership, to my way of thinking, are well worth paying, but don't forget that there are some results for which the price is far too high. Success shouldn't cost you your family, nor should your family pay the price for your success. Leadership shouldn't make you sinful or insane. It shouldn't destroy the balance of your life.

MY PERSONAL NOSEDIVE

A decade ago, I went through the darkest time of my adult life. Just as we reached the height of Southeastern's postturnaround ascent, I went into a personal nosedive that threatened my marriage and my leadership. It was a classic case of executive burnout. For me, it was an eclipse of the sun.

Success can be toxic. You need to know that. Not just hear it or read it—know it. My life stretched out thinner and thinner as though it was the surface of a balloon that was ever inflating. The problem was that I lost touch with my own core connection on the inside. My deep love for my God and my wife became compromised. I became an angry, dark soul at home. I made bad choices and barely held serious depression at bay. In public, I hid my loneliness and torment. At home I didn't.

I wasn't the first executive to experience the toxic syndrome of outward success and inner failure. Tragically, I won't be the last. What I now know is that you can turn it around. By the grace of God and with a loving wife, I got through it. A wise counselor helped. A couple of true friends were indispensible. There were many days when bailing out was a temptation. It certainly looked easier than hacking on through a dark jungle of depression. The time and resources spent striving for restoration were demanding. But hack we did. Now that I am through it and on the other side, I am grateful for what I learned.

Someone once said that in leadership the only thing worse than failure is success. The thinner you are stretched on the surface, the more toxic your inner life becomes. Don't be deceived about this.

Are you spending most of your leadership energy on the outside? Then go back on the inside. Remember those things that are real. Hold to them. Do them again. Carve out time for your soul, your true self, and your most precious relationships. You've heard all this before, haven't you? Can you hear it now from an executive who peered into the abyss and found light on the other side?

Marriages on the brink can be turned around. Some of the tools needed are the same ones needed for turning around a company or a college. Institutional reality, for example. Before a marriage can be turned around, reality must be faced. How unhappy is your spouse, really? How wretched are you to live with, really? How long since you sought your self, your soul, or your God, really?

Second, the personal investment of turning the culture of a company is not unlike turning the culture of a marriage. Brittle relationships and damaged hearts can be turned by the emotional investment of leadership. Kindness. Humility. Servanthood. They are expensive and require deep investment. Remember, in a turnaround there is no substitute for the personal expenditure of the leader.

When the leader's internal self-culture and the leader's home culture are damaged, it will tax the leader to make the turnaround. The leader's spouse can't fix it alone, and a new spouse is just buying new china and still eating takeout. The leader, who to his personal and his home's detriment has poured himself almost entirely into changing the culture of an organization, must now accept a greater role. You are the Chief Culture Officer of your home. Is that culture damaged by anger, hurt, or other personal failure? It is not too late. It can be healed and turned around, but it will cost you—personally.

The main thing it will cost you is time. That precious and limited commodity, which too many executive leaders spend in all of life's *elsewheres*, must be reallocated. There is no quick way to turn a home's culture from toxicity to wholeness. Time is medicine, and it works—but often at what feels like an excruciatingly slow pace.

Companies, colleges, and countries can be turned around. So can a life and a home. It's expensive and humbling and time-consuming. But it is worth it.

CARING FOR YOUR ART

I know I've talked a lot in this book about systems and methods and policies. But in the end, leadership is a human activity. None of the methods I've discussed will amount to anything if your leadership doesn't grow out of your own inner health. If your marriage is a disaster, if the way you relate to your employees becomes more important to you than the way you relate to your kids, if your personal integrity rises and falls according to how things are going in your business, then you are cruising for trouble at work and at home. No amount of success at the office can make up for inner emptiness and pain. That can sabotage your lifework in the blink of an eye. Trust me.

Leadership has a way of shaping you into something other than what you ought to be. Its ever-growing demands stretch you at the surface, like that ever-inflating balloon I've mentioned. Being self-aware and vigilant to monitor your inner self is nonnegotiable. You have to have more going on inside than just air. You have to develop something substantial and meaningful—a rich inner life that keeps you in balance. Unshakable values keep you even-keeled. Protect yourself and your family to preserve what makes you human and whole. Protect your art.

This leads to the most important truth I have learned about staying healthy as a leader. Stay free in God's hand. There was only one thing that kept me sane during those hard years I spent as pastor of Calvary Church. Every Sunday morning as I walked to the pulpit I prayed, "Lord, I didn't ask for this position, and I don't have to have it. If today is the day to leave it, I'm good with that." That realization kept me loose. It kept me from acting out of fear. It made it possible for me to make hard decisions. When I made mistakes, that liberty made it possible for me to keep going. Of course I preferred success to failure, but I did not live in fear of failure.

If your sense of self is completely tied up in your role as leader of your organization, you won't be able to keep a loose hold on your position. What we grasp most tightly becomes deformed. You will start to fail, and you may ride that failure all the way to the ground in a fiery crash.

If one part of turnaround leadership is hanging on, pressing through, not giving up before the mission is accomplished, another part is knowing when to ride off into the sunset, leaving things in good order so the next leader can look like a genius.

There's a famous photograph of the Giants' quarterback Y. A. Tittle from 1964. He's kneeling in the middle of the football field, his head bowed and bloody after a vicious hit from a defensive end. Though nobody could have known it at the time, the picture depicts the effective end of Tittle's career. He had been one of the greats, leading the Giants to the championship game three times though never winning. At thirty-eight, he was really getting too old for football, but he had come back for one more try at the championship. Tittle was as tough as nails and was accustomed to playing hurt, but he never really recovered from that hit in Pittsburgh. He finished the season 2-10-2.

Everybody agreed that Y. A. Tittle had played one season too long.

When I first saw that photo, it scarred me for life. I knew right then that I didn't ever want people to say, "He should have quit last year." So when it's time to leave, I leave. I let somebody else pick up where I left off.

Your organization doesn't define you. If you can keep that in mind, you can bring your unique vision to bear on the organization you are called upon to lead. Just like my fifth-grade teacher in that mean little elementary school, may you help the people under your leadership to dream big dreams and believe in a future that is very different from the present. May you always leave the flower beds a little better than you found them.

NOTES

CHAPTER 3: MY TURNAROUND LEADERSHIP JOURNEY

1. Sir Winston Churchill, "Finest Hour" (speech at the House of Commons, June 18, 1940, following the collapse of France), www.winstonchurchill.org/learn/speeches/quotations.

CHAPTER 4: BEFORE THE NUTS AND BOLTS: LEADERSHIP AS AN ART

1. Sir Winston Churchill, November 18, 1948, http://www.nationalchurchillmuseum.org/witi-wisdom-quotes.html.

CHAPTER 5: STEP 1: FACING INSTITUTIONAL REALITY

1. *Cool Hand Luke*, directed by Stuart Rosenberg (Burbank, CA: Warner Brothers, 1967).

2. This information was obtained at the Vasa Museum.

CHAPTER 8: STEP 4: CREATING AN EXECUTABLE STRATEGY

1. General Colin Powell, *My American Journey* (New York: Random House, 1995), 35.

CHAPTER 9: STEP 5: SHIFTING CULTURE

1. Joshua Rhett Miller, "Spirit Airlines' Boss Calls Industry-High Complaint Rate 'Irrelevant,' Says Dying Veteran Should've Bought Insurance," Fox News, May 3, 2012, http://www.foxnews.com/us/2012/05/03/spirit-airlines-outpaces-competitors-regarding-passenger-complaints-statistics/.

CHAPTER 12: HIRING FOR A TURNAROUND

1. John Kotter, *Leading Change* (Boston, MA: Harvard Business Review Press, 1996), 155.

2. David Garrick, quoted in J. Vernon McGee, *Proverbs through Malachi* (Nashville: Thomas Nelson, 1983), 426.

2. George Whitefield, quoted in Stephen Tomkins, *John Wesley: A Biography* (Grand Rapids, MI: Eerdmans, 2003), 128.

CHAPTER 13: THE TROUBLING ART OF FIRING

1. *The Godfather*, directed by Francis Ford Coppola (Hollywood, CA: Paramount Pictures, 1972).

CHAPTER 14: FORMING A BOARD

1. John Kotter, *Leading Change* (Boston, MA: Harvard Business Review Press, 1996), page number unknown.

2. Jim Hatch and Jeffrey Zweig, "Strategic Flexibility—The Key to Growth," *Ivey Business Journal*, March/April 2001, http://www.iveybusinessjournal.com/topics/strategy/strategic-flexibility-the-key-to-growth.